Sound Ideas
Activities for the Percussion Circle
by Doug Goodkin

This book is based on Dr. Howard Gardner's Theory of Multiple Intelligences and his book
FRAMES OF MIND: The Theory of Multiple Intelligences.

Project Manager: Gayle Giese
Editor: Debbie Cavalier
Text Editor: Marceline Bunzey Murawski
Text Proofreader: Nadine DeMarco
Editorial Assistance: Kristina Pusey

Cover Design and Art Layout: Nancy Rehm
Photography: Drew Story

Special thanks to WEST MUSIC COMPANY
for instrument photographs on the cover.

CONTENTS

INTRODUCTION:
THE MUSICAL PLAYGROUND 3
MULTIPLE INTELLIGENCES 5
PERCUSSION INSTRUMENTS 7
HOW TO USE THIS BOOK 8
ACKNOWLEDGMENTS .9

SECTION I:
GAMES FOR CHOOSING INSTRUMENTS 10
  1. Old King Glory 11
  2. Sally Go 'Round the Sun 12
  3. Son Macaron 13
  4. Paw-Paw Patch 14
  5. Johnny Works with One Hammer 15

SECTION II:
THE MUSICAL INTELLIGENCE 16
  6. Passing Sounds—Beat 17
  7. Passing Sounds—Meter 19
  8. Passing Sounds—Multiple Beats 21
  9. Instrumental Grouping/Group Improvisation .23
10. Echo Rhythm 25
11. Call-and-Response 27
12. Question/Answer .29
13. Simultaneous Canon 31

SECTION III:
THE LINGUISTIC INTELLIGENCE 33
14. Name Rhythms 34
15. Names of Instruments 36
16. Nursery Rhyme—Bow-Wow 38
17. Percussive Poems—Gata Tumba 40
18. Percussive Poems—Son Macaron Two 42
19. Percussive Poems—Debajo de un Botón . . .44
20. Percussive Poems—Okino Taiko 46
21. Middle Eastern Drum Language 48

SECTION IV:
THE LOGICAL-MATHEMATICAL
INTELLIGENCE 51
22. Four-Level Canon 53
23. Poetic Structure 56
24. Sound Allowance .58
25. Coming Together .59

SECTION V:
THE VISUAL-SPATIAL INTELLIGENCE 61
26. Conductor 62
27. Instrument Shape .64
28. Instrument Sculpture 65
29. Graphic Notation .66
30. Kinesthetic Graphic Notation 68
31. Rhythmic Notation 69

SECTION VI:
THE BODILY-KINESTHETIC INTELLIGENCE . .71
32. Frame Drum Technique 72
33. Back Drumming 74
34. Blind Playing 75
35. Accompanying Dancers 76
36. Moving with Instruments 77

SECTION VII:
THE PERSONAL INTELLIGENCES 78
37. Instruments as Props 80
38. Percussive Storytelling 81
39. Preferred Instruments 82

CODA:
THE DRUMMERS IN GOLDEN GATE PARK . . .84

ABOUT THE AUTHOR 88

INTRODUCTION:
THE MUSICAL PLAYGROUND

"Look what I drew!" exclaims the proud preschooler, and admiring parents put the picture up on the refrigerator. "Want to see our play?" ask the kids at the party, and the adults stop socializing to watch it. "Look at me!" shouts the five-year-old swinging across the playground bars, and the grown-ups pause from their conversation to cheer.

These children are doing the serious work of building their multitude of intelligences through spontaneous play and self-directed work. They explore, experiment, try out, act out, improvise, and create their way into understanding how things work. They draw, work on puzzles, play with dolls and action figures, and climb the jungle gym at the playground. In short, they do all the things that children need to do to make sense of the world. Before they ever step foot in a school, they are immersed in nature's curriculum, instinctively gravitating toward activities that prepare them for the demands and delights of daily life.

Children act from instinct but are socialized by observing adult reactions to their behavior. When adults witness, encourage, admire, and applaud children's efforts, they help to build a child's sense of self-worth and accomplishment. They are also affirming the value of the activity.

Picture a child hitting a drum, or running his or her hands up and down the playground of the piano keys, or loudly singing and banging a cup to the beat of a spontaneous song. How do most adults react? "Stop that noise!" they shout. Or, "Go outside where I can't hear you!" Where is the equivalent of musical-refrigerator art? What happens to the musical impulse without adult support for the beginning steps?

We know that enough experience scribbling eventually leads to recognizable shapes and figures, that babbling is a necessary precursor to coherent speech, that clumsy walking precedes graceful skipping. It is only logical to assume that music requires a similar period of unbridled exploration, a chance to slowly transform the chaos of noise to the form and beauty of music. Simply put, children need the equivalent of a musical playground to play with sound. They need time and space to do it, actively encouraged by adult participation and free from adult rebuke.

Such musical exploration is difficult to enjoy in privacy. The child quietly working a puzzle, drawing on paper, shaping with clay, climbing a tree, or looking at a picture book is not intruding on family/community space. By contrast, the child freely exploring the sonic potential of pots and pans, struggling to produce a recognizable tone on the violin, or working out a new piano piece tests the patience (and sometimes sanity!) of fellow family members. How and where can we create an atmosphere conducive to musical play?

One place we can turn to is the schools. Since all children go to school, a music program in every school is a guarantee that all children can develop their musical intelligence. This is an easy answer to the "where." But the "how" is more problematic. Schools have a long history of separating work and play by diving in too soon to mechanics and structure without sufficient attention paid to play and exploration. Where can we find an approach that not only creates a time and space for play, but also actively guides it with the work of increased understanding, knowledge, and technical mastery?

Enter Orff-Schulwerk, a contemporary reincarnation of our ancient need to play, sing, and dance brought into the school community under the heading of innovative music education. It begins from the premise that music is closer to us than we imagine, brought to life by such simple tools as the rhythm of our name, the sounds of the alphabet, the snap of a finger, or the jingle of a tambourine. If we can think of such elements as the jigsaw puzzles of sound, allow ourselves to play and work our way through to increased coherence of expression, we might reclaim that vital ground of babble before speech, play before work, and experiment before fact that is sorely lacking in children's musical development.

The materials at our disposal are simple and close at hand—our own bodies, voices, and imaginations. Following Alfred North Whitehead's injunction that "the best education extracts the utmost information from the simplest apparatus," we explore the sounds of the body and voice, the sonic potential of language, the expressive possibility of gesture and movement, and an idea—a rhythm, a rhyme, a song—thrown into the center of the ring for imaginative development.

The moment we begin such work, we will note that there is a second demand that sets music apart from dancing, Lego building, writing, or checkers. All of these activities can be done alone or with a friend. But when it comes to discovering the basics of musical composition—how sounds fit together—we need to work with more than one sound at a time. In short, we need a group to conduct our experiments.* Though there are solitary components to musical development—from the spontaneous singing that children do (an important form of musical babble before musical speech**) to free improvisation on available instruments, to the scales and pieces practiced in the formal lesson—the excitement and genius of the Schulwerk lies in the group experience; not only making music together from the very beginning, but actively improvising and creating music as a group.

Proceeding from the solid base of body, voice, and mind within the circle of the group, we venture out into the marvelous world of percussion. This book is an extension of two previous books with Warner Bros. Publications, *Name Games* and *A Rhyme in Time,* which deal with the compositional possibilities of language. While all the activities in those books can be transposed to percussion ensemble, these games and exercises grew from the expressive potential of the instruments themselves. They are built both as musical playgrounds for the children to romp about freely, swinging on the jungle gyms of sound, and as musical laboratories in which to conduct serious experiments and test the results—how do these two sounds and patterns fit together and react? Both are equipped with simple apparatus usable by untrained hands, a group with which to try things out and a teacher trained in guiding it all. Following Carl Orff's injunction "Let the children be their own composers," the accent is consistently on the compositional potential of an idea.

---

* There are other ways to accomplish that, but the training and patience required to coordinate two hands on the piano will be too frustrating for the child ready to make music *now,* and the multitrack tape recorder is a too expensive, unwieldy, and unchildlike solution.

** See Patricia Shehan Campbell's book: *Songs in Their Heads: Music and Its Meaning in Children's Lives*: Oxford University Press, 1998.

MULTIPLE INTELLIGENCES

A look at the table of contents reveals a subtext in this book's content—the possibility of using Howard Gardner's Theory of Multiple Intelligences as a gathering focus. First published in 1983 in his book *Frames of Mind: The Theory of Multiple Intelligences*, Gardner's theory challenged the notion that intelligence is a singular noun. Based on his own experience in education, recent discoveries in neuroscience, and a survey of related literature, he suggested that every person has not one, but at least seven, different types of intelligences: Linguistic; Musical; Logical-Mathematical; Visual-Spatial; Body-Kinesthetic; Intrapersonal; and Interpersonal.* Further descriptions of each are given at the beginning of each section. Every intelligence follows its own developmental path and internal logic, but is also inextricably intertwined with the others.

Seen through this lens, music is never simply music alone—it is math made audible, language sung, architecture unthawed, gestures sounded, social relationships revealed in sound, and emotions expressed in pitch and rhythm. Conversely, we can reverse all the above—math is silent music, language both sound and sense, architecture is frozen music.

What does this theory offer our notions of schools and our practices of effective teaching? Pedagogically speaking, it helps us recognize that every subject calls upon a blend of intelligences. Children given exercise in each intelligence are better equipped to understand the larger picture of education. Multiple intelligence theory also affirms the importance of arts education. Seen as incidental to the three R's by people who have never experienced its deep connections, the arts are in a constant defensive posture in our schools. By elevating music to an intelligence rather than its traditional title of a talent, skill, aptitude, or recreational pastime, Gardner brings it firmly into the business of a school's curriculum.

But here we encounter a problem. When teachers who have been educated through two or three intelligences seek to apply this information to curriculum, their efforts are invariably short-sighted and superficial. In many of the presentations I have seen, educators simply don't know how music fits in beyond learning math facts to a beat or singing a song about social relations.

Orff-Schulwerk began from the other direction, beginning as an intuitive artistic practice exploring the deep structural connections of music with other fields. My own excitement about Gardner's work came from recognizing a theory that gave language to the experiences I was already having in my classroom. The games presented here were not invented to prove or activate multiple intelligences—they grew organically from an imaginative way of working and then seemed to fit comfortably into that framework. They offer tangible evidence of ways in which intelligences are both separate and interconnected. As such, they may be of use and interest to teachers in any field.

* Gardner has since researched two other intelligences. This book will concern itself with the original seven presented in his initial work.

The Music Specialist and the Classroom Teacher

The activities presented here are neither the spontaneous play of children nor the measured exercises of adults, but a bridge between the two. They aim to infect the routine of adult exercise with the spirit of child's play and, likewise, to temper the raw spontaneous musical response with the requirements of form and pattern. They are offered as *ideas* for group composition and improvisation that are concrete, understandable, tangible, and tactile. As music teachers, our primary concern is to awaken, nurture, and develop the musical intelligence. Following Duke Ellington's dictate, "if it sounds good, it is good," the musical result is the measure of success.

These activities help children witness the natural confluence of intelligences called upon in the music classroom. Classroom teachers may be delighted to discover that they can enter the room of music through the door of more familiar subjects—math, language, art, and more. Unlike the musical specialist, they may use the musical activity to introduce, reinforce, invigorate, or embellish a math or language idea. As such, each activity offers suggestions for classroom applications. The ideal integrated school would have music specialists using these activities for musical purposes and classroom teachers using the same or similar activities for language, math, or other purposes.

Most lessons include a heading, "Music extension," with suggested listening examples and reflective activities. Since a main focus of these games is to introduce the various compositional possibilities of how sounds go together, it is exciting to connect the children to examples from the world of already composed music. The failure of music appreciation classes comes from a lack of context. Once children are involved in compositional activities like those presented here, they have a natural curiosity for hearing other examples and a context for listening. Though children making music is always the primary strategy of effective music education, reflection, analysis, and listening should not be neglected. Such extensions help complete the loop of the ideas introduced.

The ideas given in this book are mere suggestions—some I have not used with the activity. The intention is to point to some ways the games and activities can be reinforced—you the teacher must choose from your own repertoire and from within the context of your goals and themes for study.

Most lessons also include the heading, "Classroom application," to give the teacher ways to modify the ideas to his or her own goals and activities. This gives both the music specialist and classroom teacher concrete models for the collaboration suggested above. Again, I have not experienced all of these classroom extensions and where I couldn't imagine one, I left it out. These suggestions point the way toward an integrated curriculum that gives the child a chance to witness the interconnection of all subjects. Dividing the day into math class, music class, reading, and recess is a useful fiction for the convenience of school systems, schedules, and focused study, but at root, they are all intertwined.

PERCUSSION INSTRUMENTS

Orff-Schulwerk requires us to understand how much music can be made with our three essentials: body, voice, and mind. Yet mention the word "music" and instruments spring instantly to mind. Is clapping a form of primitive drumming or drumming the outgrowth of clapping? Is the voice imitating the violin or the violin imitating the voice? Logic dictates that the egg of music in the body/voice hatches into the chicken of instrumental music. The Orff class tends to follow this logic, preparing the instrumental work through body percussion, singing, and movement. Yet the distance between the egg and the musical egg shaker is small. Since the purpose of music is to speak all those things that can't be said in words, numbers, pictures, or movements, anything that expands the expressive possibilities of the hand and tongue is welcomed early on.

For young children delighted in discovering what marvelous music mere clapping and vocalizing can make, the transfer to the technical demands of a piano or violin is too daunting. They need something more immediate, and here is where percussion instruments form the ideal starter set for instrumental exploration. They are affordable, portable, storable, easily playable at the beginning level, and offer a wide palette of tone color and playing techniques. Though children see the value and delight of clapping, moving, and speaking rhythmically, the enchantment of extending their voices through the chime of the triangle, the sharp retort of the woodblock, and the boom of the bass drum increases their pleasure, excitement, and motivation.

The activities in this book are based on an unusual musical premise—instruments are interchangeable. It is rare to find music separate from the specific instruments that play them (Bach's *Art of the Fugue* comes to mind), but these activities are independent from specific orchestrations and work equally well with different combinations of instruments. Indeed, one can repeat the same activity many times with a different mix of instruments and get a markedly different aesthetic result.

A classic "starter kit" contains a healthy mix of different timbres and materials: skin, wood, and metal, as well as different playing techniques, such as shakers, scrapers, instruments struck together, and instruments struck with sticks or mallets. Frame drums, tambourines, woodblocks, claves, cowbells, triangles, finger cymbals, maracas, and guiros are some basic percussion instruments one is likely to encounter in a music classroom. Other novelty instruments have become solid members of the music education family: the vibraslap, flexatone, and rainstick; Brazilian instruments like the agogo bell, tamborim, and ganza; Latin percussion instruments like bongos, congas, and cabasas/afuches; West African instruments like the gankogui bell, ahastse, djembe, and talking drum; Middle Eastern dumbek drums; Chinese gongs, drums, and cymbals; Australian Aboriginal clapping sticks; and the Indonesian angklung. The mix of ethnic origins is making the contemporary music classroom into a miniature United Nations of sound! This not only invites further culture study, but also encourages experimental composition as Indian tabla meets African mbira, Brazilian berimbau, and Tibetan bells.*

* See recordings of Mickey Hart, Stephan Micus, Zakir Hussain, or Don Cherry with the group Codona for examples of such mixes.

HOW TO USE THIS BOOK

This book can be used by music specialists, classroom teachers, community organizers, workshop leaders, birthday party performers—in short, wherever there is a group of people gathered who enjoy playing together. Like the material in its companion books by Warner Bros. Publications, *Name Games* and *A Rhyme in Time,* the activities presented are intended as open-ended structures to be animated by the imagination of the group. They live in the spaces between game, exercise, and piece, and can serve to introduce musical concepts, encourage improvisation, or stimulate composition.

As noted, the pieces are grouped by the particular intelligence highlighted, similar to a menu with the musical intelligence as the main course and six others as the appetizers, beverages, and desserts. Within each area, activities are grouped sequentially, following an intuitive developmental path, but here again, the teacher may choose from the menu according to his or her need in the curriculum.

Most of the activities are designed to be done in a circle. Though many are adaptable to other formations, the very formation of the circle is an integral part of the teaching style. I prefer to sit on the floor, with everyone sitting cross-legged (or in what today's students call "crisscross applesauce"). This brings us closer to the earth, creates a different feeling of intimacy, avoids the moving of chairs (and tipping over in chairs!), and sidesteps the tiresome process of children looking for their own special and different chair. That said and done, most activities work equally well in a circle of chairs or stools (indeed, if percussion such as congas are used, they are necessary).

One thing not covered here is detailed information about percussion instruments: techniques, cultural facts, or set pieces. It goes without saying that in addition to using these instruments in freely exploratory ways, children need to learn specific techniques and a repertoire of traditional pieces. This work can serve to precede, parallel, or extend those more formal percussion experiences—both are necessary to a thorough musical training.

The reader may note that no suggested age levels are given with each activity. This omission of age levels feels prudent for three reasons:
1. The variables of what different groups of kids can achieve are great—i.e., third-graders having their first Orff class are markedly different from third graders who have been involved in such a program since they were three. Kids raised in a musical family and community can accomplish quite different things than those raised by appliances.
2. The book assumes readers have sufficient teaching experience to understand the range of their grade level's interest and ability. New teachers must learn by trial and error.
3. Since so many activities are open-ended, they can be done virtually with any age, made simpler or more complex, as circumstances require.

Most activities are aimed toward the elementary-age child, with many activities that can be simplified for preschool or expanded for middle school.

ACKNOWLEDGMENTS

It is important to acknowledge that these types of ideas and activities have been floating around in the Orff community (and others as well), initiated, revised, and expanded by all of the various teachers and students involved in experimental investigation. As such, it is difficult, if not impossible, to track an idea to its source. Even when I imagine that I created an activity myself, certainly someone else has done a similar one somewhere. Furthermore, once the creative impulse is released, it takes on a life of its own, urged along by the participants.

Special thanks to the children in my classes who helped develop these ideas with their own imaginative response: to Sofía López-Ibor for her always-inspiring teaching models and for reading the manuscript and offering many valuable suggestions; to James Harding, Susan Kennedy, Wolfgang Hartmann, and Rodrigo Fernandez for sharing their own styles of imaginatively developing material; to Steve Calantropio for introducing me to "Son Macaron"; and to Judith Thomas for her ability to think clearly and "strangely."*

Now we're ready to come down from the airy flight of theory and get started with the serious play and mirthful work. Explore, experiment, enjoy!

* Orff teacher Judith Thomas's marvelous expression used to describe one of the many gifts of the Shulwerk.

SECTION I:
GAMES FOR CHOOSING INSTRUMENTS

Orff-Schulwerk is based on the premise that the process of teaching music must itself be musical. Every detail of planning a class is an opportunity to exercise the children's musicality. The following five games offer musical ways for children to choose instruments and be seated in the circle ready to try the succeeding activities. The chance nature of the games sidesteps the problem of who gets to choose instruments first, and appeals to children's sense of fair play. Games also add an element of suspense and mystery. They warm up the class, both musically and socially, for the activity to come. Once you get a feeling for how to convert existing games or songs to means of preparing the circle, feel free to invent your own.

As the children get comfortable with the process of choosing instruments and more experienced in playing them, you may wish to simply say, "Get an instrument and come to the circle." A preliminary game is certainly not necessary for every class! Yet even seasoned teachers and children will enjoy the fun of making each task of the musical class a musical opportunity.

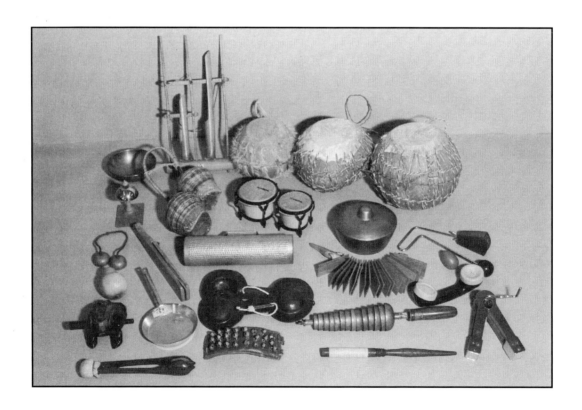

1. OLD KING GLORY

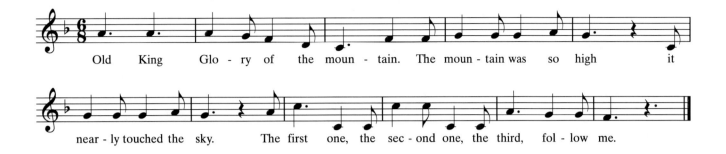

Old King Glo - ry of the moun - tain. The moun - tain was so high it

near - ly touched the sky. The first one, the sec - ond one, the third, fol - low me.

Focus: Choosing instruments

Set-up: All seated in a circle. Percussion instruments (one per child) are placed on a table or on the floor near the circle. Select instruments that are played with mallets and instruments that allow one hand to be free.

Activity:
- All sing the song while the leader marches behind the circle playing the beat (with mallet or hand) on a drum. On the words, "first one, the second one, the third, follow me," the leader taps three children in a row. Only the third gets up, quickly chooses an instrument and follows leader around the circle, playing to the beat while continuing to sing.
- The new person chooses another participant as above, who picks up an instrument and joins the line. The most recent person in line is always the new tapper.
- Continue until the last person has joined the line. Sing one more time, marching around in a circle, change the words (and follow action) to "the first one, the second one, we all sit down!"

Variations:
- If the group is large, the first, second, *and* third people can all get up to follow the leader.
- The leader can also be the leader each time instead of the most recent person in line.

Comments:
This is one of my favorite games to play with preschoolers. It's a marvelous living illustration of the law of conservation of matter—as the line gets bigger, the circle gets smaller—until it disappears! Then we sing one more time, sit down at the end and presto!—the circle has come back. It's also a great game to teach the discipline of inhibiting response—when kids are tapped first and second, they naturally want to get up. It takes practice to realize that only the third may get up!

Marching to the beat and playing an instrument while singing is quite an integration of tasks. It is also great fun, and the children will dive in with gusto. You may need to remind them to play softer and sing louder. The children will be so involved in the game that they will not be consciously working on their rhythmic skills. This is a good opportunity to observe each child's natural inclination for cohesive, integrated rhythm. At the beginning stages, corrections must be delicately made with sensitivity to the flow of the game. Stopping the game to correct each child disturbs the rhythm of the game itself and might make the child overly self-conscious. A simple statement might get the point across: "I loved the way that Abby played the same beat that she was walking. Abby, can you show us how you did that? Let's all try it."

Though there are many variations and marvelous classroom extensions of this game, the purpose here, as noted, is simply to get the kids seated in the circle, each with a percussion instrument—and thus, ready to try any of the other activities in the book.

2. SALLY GO 'ROUND THE SUN

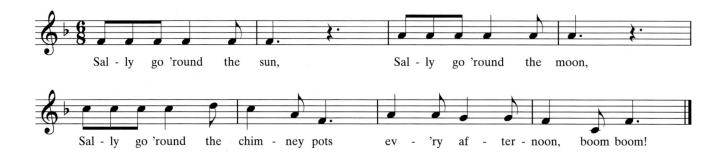

Sal - ly go 'round the sun, Sal - ly go 'round the moon,

Sal - ly go 'round the chim - ney pots ev - 'ry af - ter - noon, boom boom!

Focus: Choosing instruments

Set-up: Instruments are set out in a circle before the children enter class.

Activity:
- Give a clear direction that no one may touch the instruments during the first activity. (If necessary, make a game out of it—anyone who touches is "out.") Everyone follows the leader, who is weaving in and out of the instruments. All are singing the song.
- Continue until all are inside the circle of instruments—all sit down on "boom boom!"
- Leader turns around and picks up the instrument behind him or her, and gestures to the next in line to do the same, until all have an instrument.
- Sing the song again while seated, gesturing beat in the air and playing instruments on "boom boom!"
- As above, but play beat lightly on instrument while singing and accenting "boom boom!"

Variations:
- Sing the song while marching, reversing directions on "boom boom!"
- As above, but crouch on "boom boom!" Change song to "Pop Goes the Weasel" and all jump up on the word "Pop." Resume singing and marching "Sally."
- Leader is inside the circle going the other way. The leader stops and points to someone on "boom boom!" That person plays an eight-beat solo on the instrument before the song and marching start again (with soloist as new pointer).

Comments:
This is another favorite game of the young ones. The game not only leads them to an instrument, it also gives them a chance to practice playing a steady beat softly. They will naturally enjoy playing the "boom boom!" accent.

3. SON MACARON

Son mac-a-ron son Fe - ri - on. Ma-ri-on, Ma-ri-on, Le-ah, Le-ah, tip tip tip,

Le - ah, Le - ah, tap tap tap. One beat, two beat, three beat *catch!*

Focus: Choosing instruments
Beat-passing game

Set-up: All are seated with palms up, right hand on top of left hand of neighbor to the right.

Activities:

- While singing the song, the leader crosses over body with right hand to clap the right hand of neighbor to the left, who then passes the beat to the neighbor to the left, and so on around the circle. On the word "catch," the person about to receive the beat tries to pull his or her hand away so as not to get tapped. If tapped, he or she is out.
- Whoever is "out" chooses an instrument and stands behind the circle, playing one of the following choices: "tip tip tip," "tap tap tap," "one beat, two beat, three beat," or "catch!"
- Continue until all are out. Play the song one more time in the circle and sit down on "catch!"

Variations:

- While passing the beat, the rhythm of "tip tip tip" and "tap tap tap" may be played on the hand on which they arrive.
- Above rhythms may be passed across three hands, one for each word.
- For variations with instruments, see "Son Macaron Two" in the Linguistic Intelligence section.

Comments:

Clapping your hands to the steady beat is one level of beat competency, and feeling the beat in a group and clapping one beat when your turn comes up is another level. This game requires alertness, attention, and a strong internalized sense of beat. It also serves two practical questions well: 1) How to choose instruments; 2) What to do with the children who get "out" in a game.

4. PAW-PAW PATCH

Where, oh where is lit - tle Su - sie? Where, oh where is lit - tle Su - sie?

Where, oh where is lit - tle Su - sie? Way down yon-der in the paw - paw patch.

Focus: Choosing instruments

Set-up: Instruments in a visible and accessible place. Children are seated as partners, one called the "puppy," the other the "kitten."

Activities:

- All sing song, substituting "puppy" or "kitten" for the name in the song. All the "puppies" leave the circle and touch an instrument that follows the teacher's direction, as in "Touch an instrument made of wood." They must return to the circle by the end of the song.
- Repeat as above with "kittens."
- Continue with different directions: "Touch an instrument: one made of metal; one that you can shake to make sound; one that you can scrape; one that makes a long sound; one that makes a loud sound; etc."
- As above, but "puppies" choose a special motion and pathway to reach the instrument and return to their place. Next time, "kittens" must copy the motion and pathway. Switch.
- Sing the song using each child's name in turn. This time, the child chosen picks up the instrument and returns with it to the circle. That child can sing the next child's name. While seated in the circle with instruments waiting for others to choose, children may accompany the song.

Variations:

- While seated in circle, "puppies" may sing the song, each accompanying with their own idea. "Kitten" partners must copy the rhythm the next time, singing the song.
- As above, with "kittens" first.

Comments:

This text is not recommended for older children. Though it's tempting to suggest substituting more hip lyrics *(Where, oh where are the super-cool dudes?),* finding a more age-appropriate song is probably a better choice.

5. JOHNNY WORKS WITH ONE HAMMER

John - ny works with one ham - mer, one ham - mer, one ham - mer.

John - ny works with one ham - mer. Now he works with two.

Focus: Choosing instruments

Set-up: Instruments in a semicircle, one for each child. Children are off to the side in line.

Activity:

- All sing first verse of song while first child in line plays the beat on the first instrument on one side of the semicircle. At the end of the first verse, all clap the rhythm of the last two phrases: *"Johnny works with one hammer, now he works with two."*

  During the clapping, the first child goes to second instrument, and the next child in line goes to the first instrument. Note that the children do not pick up the instruments. Repeat song with second verse: *"Johnny works with two hammers...."*

- Repeat as above as children gradually join in and move around the circle.

Variations:

- If the class is large, children may get tired of singing the song (*"Johnny works with 23 hammers, 23 hammers, 23 hammers..."*). In this case, all think the words to the song without actually singing, while continuing to play the beat.
- Substitute a girl's name or a gender-neutral name for Johnny.
- Substitute the name of each new player.

Comments:

This way of choosing instruments has the added advantage of many people getting to play different instruments before the next activity begins. Certainly the last person will notice that he or she did not get to play as many. In this case, tell the children to remember their line order and promise to go in reverse order during the next class. (If you forget, they'll remind you!)

This structure is a lesson in texture, with the size and variety of sound growing with each repetition. (As in Ravel's "Bolero." If you have the recording, you might play it for the children and discuss and compare to "Johnny Works With One Hammer.")

SECTION II: THE MUSICAL INTELLIGENCE

This group of activities speaks directly to the task of awakening, nurturing and developing the musical intelligence. My interpretation of this intelligence is as follows:

- The capacity to perceive the aural world accurately; hear the "music" of all sounds.
- The capacity to hear, imitate, transform, and create beat, rhythm, and rhythmic patterns.
- The capacity to hear, imitate, transform, and create pitch, melody, and melodic patterns.
- The capacity to hear, imitate, transform, and create nuances of expression—timbre, accent, dynamics, tempo, and ornamentations.
- The capacity to hear, imitate, transform, and create musical texture, following more than one musical thought at a time, and keeping one's place when performing in ensemble.

Here's how someone with an advanced musical intelligence may experience the world:

> As a child, the drawing room became my paradise. Half in fun, half in earnest, I learned to know the keys by their names and with my back to the piano I would call the notes of any chord, even the most dissonant one. From then on, it became mere 'child's play' to master the intricacies of the keyboard, and I was soon able to play first with one hand, later with both, any tune that caught my ear.
>
> —Anton Rubinstein

An activity relying on the musical intelligence speaks directly to the ear, bypassing any visual representation, numerical counting, verbal aids, or technical details, most of the strategies of the traditional piano lesson. (It is striking how little such lessons call directly upon the musical intelligence in teaching music!) The sounds and nothing but the sounds must be heard, imitated, transformed, and created anew. The classic echo rhythm is a case in point. The leader claps a rhythm, students listen, and then they clap back. Later, a rhythm clapped may be transformed by performing the same rhythm divided between clapping and patting. New patterns are created when the given rhythm becomes a "question" and the students must create their own "answer."

Though some of the activities in this section cross into nonmusical strategies, most rely primarily on the ear as the organ of perception and mastery.

6. PASSING SOUNDS—BEAT

Focus: Musical Intelligence

Concept: Sequence
              Timbre

Set-up: Unless otherwise noted, this and all succeeding activities begin with a random selection of percussion instruments in a circle, one per child.

Activity:
- All freely explore instruments simultaneously to discover different sounds and playing techniques, and then choose one sound/technique to share with the group.
- Each shares sound in turn around the circle.
- As above, but as a "wave"—second person starts playing before first person ends, third before second ends (first should finish when third is playing; i.e., it's the responsibility of the first player to end soon after the second joins in).
- As above, but with an underlying steady beat. When the beat returns to the first person, all play one more sound together.
- As above, turning to the next person and making eye contact while passing beat. Following the last beat (when the beat returns to the first person), all play with energy focused toward the center of the circle.
- Repeat above going in the other direction.
- Twice through, once to the left and then to the right.
- As above, with eyes closed.
- Sing a song or recite a rhyme while passing the beat, ending on the last word. ("Twinkle Little Star," "Son Macaron," etc.)

Variations:
- Pass in different pattern, alternating left and right as shown:

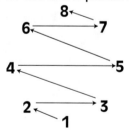

- Send in one direction. Anyone can send back in the other direction through eye contact and directional gesture, i.e., playing with body facing or leaning toward the next person.
- As above, changing direction by playing two eighth notes.
- Pass anywhere in the circle with eye contact and directional gesture.

Music extension:
There are a few examples I know of in which music is played in a circle, as above:
1. "Pounding Millet." A recording of women pounding grain in a giant mortar in which they coordinate their motions so the sticks don't collide. CD titled *The Fulani: Music from Niger and Northern Benin*: Unesco Collection; D 8006.
2. "Bambu Beat." Though the rhythms are more complex than the mere beat, the Venezuelan bamboo tubes called "quitiplas" follows a similar style—three interlocking rhythms. CD titled *Keith Terry and Crosspulse, Serpentine*: Ubiquity CPR CD001.

Classroom application:
Practice rote information: days of the week, months of the year, math facts, rhyming words, and

so on, using the formula of taking turns around the circle to the beat.

Comments:
One may ask why this exercise is included under musical intelligence when it requires many visual/spatial and sequential skills for success. One answer is that it reveals the inward sense of beat as each person plays in turn. A second has to do with evoking the capacity to "hear the music of all sounds." As the beat is passed, each one is expressed on a different percussion instrument with its own unique timbre. The random grouping of sounds that precede and follow each other creates an automatic orchestration that is often charming, filled with slight variations (two cowbells next to each other pitched slightly apart) and great contrasts (a drum, triangle, woodblock, and shaker all in a row). Watch the faces of the children and see how they respond—do the groupings give them musical satisfaction or do they feel like random sounds? Guide them by asking leading questions: "Where in the circle do you think the song sounds the most interesting? Any suggestions about switching the order? Do you feel any special groupings of the beats?"

7. PASSING SOUNDS—METER

Focus: Musical Intelligence

Concept: Meter

Set-up: Instruments grouped in patterns of 3, 4, 5, or 6.

Activity:

- Choose a rhyme to fit the instrument groupings and pass the beat within that group while reciting:

- As above, using a grouping of three with a text in 3/4 meter:

Variations:

- As above, with students forming their own metrical groupings and choosing accompanying rhymes.
- Explore accents within meters, as in 5/4 divided 3-2 or 2-3, 8/4 divided 3-3-2, etc.
- Explore meters with and without texts with random groupings of instruments, creating groupings through awareness of accents. In the following example, instruments in bold are accented:

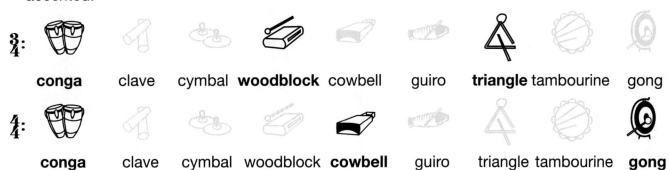

- The most strictly musical of tasks is the last variation: listening for the strong/weak patterns of different meters and responding accordingly. This last variation is particularly interesting if the number of players doesn't match the given meter, as in nine players passing around a four-beat meter. After the first time around the circle, different instruments will play the accent.

In this example, it will take four times around the circle before the pattern repeats:

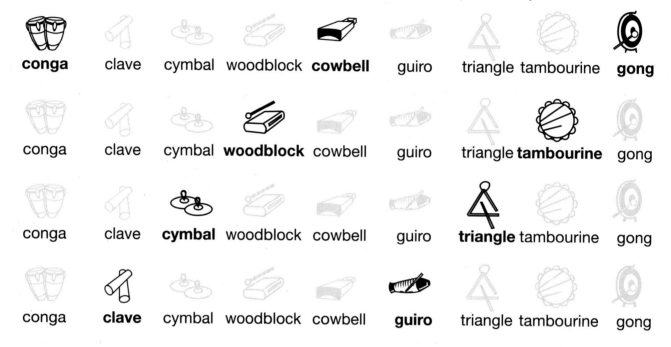

Music extension:
Play game following meters of select recorded music ("Blue Danube Waltz," "Take Five," and so on.)

Classroom application:
Transfer accent idea to list idea, as in accenting months with 31 days.

Comments:
Arranging the instruments as described makes the experience of meter both visual and aural. The addition of text brings language into play as well. Words, patterns, sounds, visual grouping, group coordination—time and again, our efforts here to showcase one intelligence at a time are thwarted by the Orff practice of seamless integration!

8. PASSING SOUNDS—MULTIPLE BEATS

Focus: Musical Intelligence

Concept: Rhythmic texture

Activity:

- Review Game 6: Passing Sounds—Beat. When beat reaches halfway around the circle, send another one.

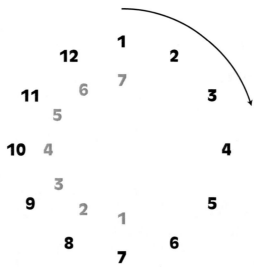

- Send three or more beats around circle.

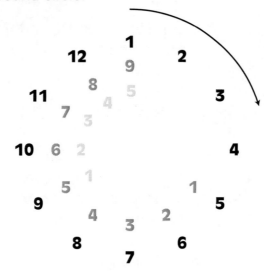

- Send beat in opposite directions at once (beats will cross halfway through the circle and should continue back to the beginning).

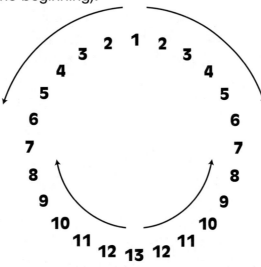

- Each player plays two beats around the circle before passing it on.

(1   1   2   2   3   3 etc.)

- Each player plays three beats. Four beats. Also a good way to introduce the meter of Game 7.

Variations:

- Send four beats around the circle and somewhere past the halfway point, send two. The two beats will start to "catch up" with the four beats. After some experimental passes, figure out precisely when to send it so that all will arrive back to start without "crossing."

1	1	1	1	2	2	2	2	3	3	3	3	4	4	4	4	5	5	5	5	6	6	6	6	7	7	7	7	8	8	8	8	9	9	9	9	10	10	10	10	1
																				1	1	2	2	3	3	4	4	5	5	6	6	7	7	8	8	9	9	10	10	1

- As above, sending two beats first and then one beat.
- Send four, then two, then one.
- Send four, then three, two, one.

1	1	1	1	2	2	2	2	3	3	3	3	4	4	4	4	5	5	5	5	6	6	6	6	7	7	7	7	8	8	8	8	9	9	9	9	10	10	10	10	1
				1	1	1	2	2	2	3	3	3	4	4	5	5	5	6	6	6	7	7	7	8	8	8	9	9	9	10	10	10	1							
																				1	1	2	2	3	3	4	4	5	5	6	6	7	7	8	8	9	9	10	10	1
																														1	2	3	4	5	6	7	8	9	10	1

Classroom application:
Begin sending one thing around (months of year) and then begin another (days of the week).

Comments:
This game requires sharp attention skills! In passing the beat to the left, the natural tendency is to continue looking left to visually track the beat's progress. In this game, each player must be ready to receive the next beat from the right after passing it to the left. There will be much laughter as children are "caught" not paying attention. Be sure to keep the atmosphere light and immediately discourage the other children from calling undue attention to the error.

The variation of sending two beats followed by one came up spontaneously in a recent class and delighted me with the drama of watching the one beat chasing after the two beats. The attention quotient rises considerably here, especially for the people near the end of the sequence who receive the one beat immediately after their two beats.

Musically, the two-, three-, and four-beat patterns create a different effect, and the two or more beats simultaneously effortlessly create duets, trios, etc.

9. INSTRUMENTAL GROUPING/GROUP IMPROVISATION

Focus: Musical Intelligence

Concept: Complementary patterns
Instrument grouping (classification)

Activity:
- All choose a percussion instrument and form a circle.
- All begin playing and walk slowly into center of the circle with eyes closed. Find like instruments and group skin instruments, shakers, metal instruments, etc. At given signal, open eyes and return to larger circle with the group.
- Each group plays briefly to define themselves. Adjust accordingly. (If there are any "one-of-a-kind" instruments, they form a "one-of-a-kind" group, as in vibraslap, flexatone, and bicycle horn.)
- Discuss basis for classification. (Timbre? Material? Size? Technique? Shape?)
- Without talking beforehand, each group performs a short improvisation that must have a clear beginning, middle, and end. For the beginning, one person simply begins playing. For the middle, others relate to opening statement. For the ending, all have to watch and listen for when the piece feels like it has naturally finished. Pieces can be metered, conversational, or a combination. Continue around the circle until all groups have performed.
- Talk about the improvisations. What worked well? What didn't and why? How were they different from one another?

Variations:
- Once grouped, pass beat (one per group) as in Game 6.
- Predetermine a different classification: shape, size, etc. Proceed as above.

Music extension:
- Study classification systems: woodwind, brass, strings, percussion/idiophones, membranophones, chordophones, aerophones. Classify all school instruments according to one system, both on paper and when laying them out in the room.
- Research origins of instruments and the mixture of instruments in different ensembles: Balinese gamelan, Taiko drum ensemble, jazz quartet, samba batteria, and so on.

Classroom application:
- Discuss as a class the experience of improvising together. What was necessary? How did you know who was leading and who following? How did you know when to end?
- Compare this classification system to others: plants, animals, food groups, transportation, etc.

Comments:
This exercise has duel objectives—creating music by listening and responding, and introducing musical instrument classification. The first objective goes to the heart of the musical intelligence—put a sound or rhythm out in the air (beginning), respond to it with the whole of one's musicality (middle), and listen for when it feels finished (end).

The rules of "beginning, middle, end" serve as a definition of music itself. We live in a sea of sound, and what we call music has to do both with how we organize that sound and how we frame it. The beginning and the end are the aural equivalent of the edge of the paper, separating the drawing on the paper from the table it lies on. By preceding the beginning with a moment of silence and announcing our intention, we pay a different kind of attention to the first sound, separating it in our minds from the random sounds around us. Though the person may have made the same sound earlier in the class, it is now invested with a special weight and power. We are attending to it with musical ears. John Cage built a short piece around this idea titled "4:33." The performer sits quietly for four minutes thirty-three seconds and then leaves. The sounds heard in the auditorium in the interval are the piece! Music is what we intend to hear, and is indeed always around us if we pause to listen with musical ears.

The middle is the more formal human element of music-making: the willful organization of sound through a combination of basic principles—common beats, contrasting rhythms, calls-and-responses, dynamic changes—the whole arsenal of musical communication devices and strategies. Bringing to life our initial supposition that everyone is musical, anyone can participate in this activity and show us how he or she thinks musically. For teachers responsible for knowing their students' developmental stages and tracking their progress, such an activity reveals much about the children's level of musical thinking without them feeling like they're being tested.

The end is the delicious moment when the human will, directing the show, leaves space for the piece itself to participate. If you listen to someone talking on the phone, you can hear the moment when the conversation feels like it is drawing to a close. So much in our modern world ends dictated by outwardly imposed limits: the ring of the school bell, the ding of the timer, the glance at the watch. But conversation, musical and otherwise, has its own natural rhythm. The high drama in this exercise, for participants and listeners alike, is not knowing when or how it will end. That creates a quality of listening that intensifies our musical experience.

This exercise also calls upon the personal intelligences, revealing a person's character and demonstrating social skills. Who initiates the idea? Who responds? Who leads and who follows? Who wants to make the last sound?

The second focus of this game is instrument classification. The grouping of instruments gives a coherence to the improvisation, and the types of instruments themselves participate in the process, suggesting certain kinds of musical conversations. Triangles may imply long, ringing tones, while woodblocks suggest a more percussive improvisation. Once grouped, a host of other activities are available (see the many games that follow), along with an opportunity to discuss and further investigate instrument classification.

Note that Orff practice always begins from *active experience*. The quality and excitement of a discussion generated from activity is markedly different from one that proceeds from the teacher's announcement, "Today we're going to study how instruments are classified."

10. ECHO RHYTHM

Focus: Musical Intelligence

Concept: Rhythmic variation
Phrasing

Activity:
- Leader plays a four-beat rhythm, person on left echoes, next person echoes, passing the rhythm around the circle in turn.

- Leader sends a second pattern around, as in Game 8. When patterns return to the leader, leader can continue them, change them, or stop them.

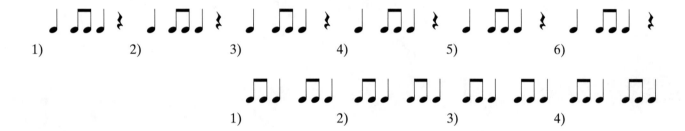

- Continue with three, four, or five patterns.
- If the group is ready, continue with one pattern for every two people.

Variations:
- As above, with phrases of varying length.
- Choose a student to be the leader that initiates the patterns.

Music extension:
Listen to examples in which echo is part of the musical fabric, from the first movement of Beethoven's "Fifth," in which a short motif from the strings is echoed by the woodwinds, to the Isley Brothers' "Twist and Shout," to the folk song "Old Texas."

Classroom application:
- Try the above game with language. (Leader: daffodils, jonquils, and so on.)
- Note the use of echo in George Herbert's poem, "Heaven."

Comments:
Echo rhythm is a classic pedagogical device that accomplishes much at once:
- It exercises the ability to imitate given rhythms.
- It reinforces a sense of beat.
- It develops understanding of phrasing.
- It builds a vocabulary of rhythms.

A little bit of echo in each class can go a long way in building rhythmic skills, especially when giving additional challenges in each new class: beginning rhythms before the downbeat, filling up the whole phrase, introducing syncopations, and so on. Remember to give each child the opportunity to lead echo over the course of the year.

11. CALL-AND-RESPONSE

Focus: Musical Intelligence

Concept: Call-and-response

Activity:
- Leader with two instruments: a drum and a whistle, the others with drums. Silently indicate whistle pointing to self, drum to the group. Leader plays this pattern as follows:

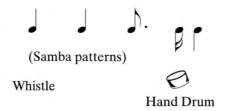

Continues until the group joins the response on the drum.

- As above, with a new pattern:

- As above, with one more:

- Review all patterns, playing the first two patterns four times each.
- Divide group into partners A and B. A does the calls (as shown above) and B does the response.
- Switch.
- Those playing the call create three-beat (first pattern) or two-beat (second pattern) variations; the response remains the same.

Variations:
Partners create their own call-and-response patterns and practice until set.

Music extension:
Listen to examples of call-and-response in various musics: Brazilian samba, sea chanteys: "Cape Cod Chantey," African-American folk songs: "Soup, Soup," "Hambone," Count Basie jazz tunes: "One O'Clock Jump," and rock tunes: "Land of a Thousand Dances," "Bo Diddley," and "Hully Gully."

Classroom application:

- Discuss difference between call-and-response and echo. In the former, the response is generally the same and expressed by the group, while the call changes and is expressed—often improvisationally—by an individual leader. Create some games to fit the form. For example, in math, the group must always answer "25" and the leader must improvise correct variations to a steady beat until he or she makes a mistake (misses the beat or gives a problem that doesn't add up to 25). The next person in the circle becomes the new leader.

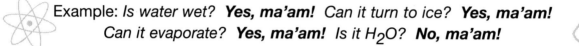

  Example: *5x5!* **25**   *24 +1!* **25**   *30-5!* **25**   *25% of 100!* **25**

- As above, with a chosen scientific topic.

  Example: *Is water wet?* **Yes, ma'am!** *Can it turn to ice?* **Yes, ma'am!**
  Can it evaporate? **Yes, ma'am!** *Is it H_2O?* **No, ma'am!**

- Both of the above games become more interesting if the group is responsible for listening carefully and noticing when the question is wrong by changing the response (No, ma'am!).

  Example: *Can it evaporate?* **Yes, ma'am!** *Is it H_2O_2?* **No, ma'am!**

Comments:

The call-and-response form is a marvelous social device used in many cultures. It is based on the model that when a situation, gesture, or phrase "calls," there is an agreed-upon ritual "response." Someone says, "How are you?" and we respond, "Fine." The teacher asks a question and our hands go up. The school bell rings and we gather our books. A bell rings in a Japanese Zen monastery and the monks all bow. The Haitian storyteller says "Cric" and the group answers "Crac."

Call-and-response songs and phrases are a fun and effective way to focus group energy, more spirited than a bell and more effective than shouting "Quiet!" They also serve a deeper purpose, acting as a kind of social glue that binds the community together. Knowing the correct response gives children a sense of security and belonging and also gives the group a sense of identity. Social grace is a learned skill, and call-and-response, both musical and otherwise, is a fine way to help teach it.

12. QUESTION/ANSWER

Focus: Musical Intelligence

Concept: Improvisation

Activity:
- Leader plays an eight-beat rhythm (question), group improvises an eight-beat rhythm (answer).

- Leader plays question on drum, rhythm sticks; each percussion group (shakers, drums, etc.) answers.
- Go around the circle one at a time: one person asks "question," next gives "answer." That person asks next "question" and so on, around the circle. Select successful dialogues as models, in which there is a relationship between the question and answer, i.e., the answer quotes part of the question

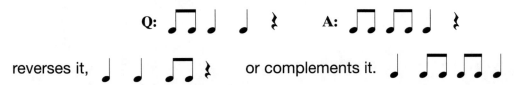

- Each person gives own question and answer, creating a 16-beat phrase.

Variations:
- Phrases of different lengths.
- Leader gives four-beat question, group eight-beat answer. Eight-beat question, four-beat answer. Five-beat question, three-beat answer, etc.

- Partners/small groups create own question/answer game.

Music extension:
- Listen to examples of question/answer phrases in jazz ("Wrap Your Troubles in Dreams" from *California Here I Come,* Bill Evans, Eddie Gomez, Philly Joe Jones: Verve; VE 2-2545), and classical Indian music ("Talawadyam Kaccheri" from *Karnatic: A Panorama of South Indian Music*: Everyman; SRV•73011).
- Set and notate successful 16-beat question/answer phrases. Use as a starting point for a composition.

Classroom application:
- Create verbal models of question/answer relationships:
  - Quoting: "What is 5 times 5?" "5 times 5 is 25."
  - Matching: "What did you get when you went to the store?" "I bought some peanuts and a few things more."
  - Complementing: "When was the War of 1812?" "I don't know."
- Apply question/answer concept to poetry: Ferlingetti's "The World Is a Beautiful Place."

Comments:

This exercise offers endless variations. It can be prepared first through body percussion, nonsense speech, and real questions and answers set in a rhythmic framework "What did you eat for breakfast today?" "Scrambled eggs, toast, and a glass of O.J." (extra credit for rhyming!) Such activities help break down the mystique of improvisation. The exercise can also begin freely, with questions and answers of any length, mirroring actual speech. The four- to eight-beat exercise over a steady pulse offers important limits to house the improvisation, but can also be musically stifling if used exclusively. Most music is not so predictably symmetrical— make sure you try some of the phrase length variations.

13. SIMULTANEOUS CANON

Focus: Musical Intelligence

Concept: Multiple imitation

Activity:
- Leader gives rhythm, group echoes. While the group echoes, the leader gives the next rhythm. Continue in this fashion.

- Leader gives the first rhythm. As the group echoes, the next person in the circle gives the next rhythm. As the group echoes that rhythm, the next person gives the new rhythm. Continue around the circle.

Variations:
As above, in partners.

Music extension:
Transfer a set sequence to notation.

Classroom application:
- Transfer the above to color and design.

- Transfer to real speech between partners:
1) It is hot.	I am tired.	This is strange.	When will it end?	Here comes the teacher.
2)	It is hot.	I am tired.	This is strange.	When will it end?

- As above, in question/answer format.
1) What is your name?	How old are you?	When is your birthday?	Can I have some gum?
2)	My name is Fred.	I am 10 years old.	July 15th.

1) 5 x 5	6 x 6	7 x 7	8 x 8	9 x 9	8 x 8	8 x 8	8 x 8	8 x 8	Finally!
2)	25	36	49	65	81	65	65	64	64

- Apply these models to the issue of developing listening skills.

Comments:

This is a challenging exercise for any age level, in which the input and output occur simultaneously. I don't know the exact neuroscience of this, but you can imagine something pretty interesting is going on with the firing patterns in the brain—like the grand finale of the 4th of July when they set all the fireworks off at once! Though research confirms that attention is not an isolated skill that can be mastered and applied over all subject areas, this exercise gives the student a taste of what it feels like to *really* pay attention and can be used as a reference point.

Note that this is also a difficult exercise for the *teacher* to lead. It helps to keep the rhythms simple and change the timbre, as in this example:

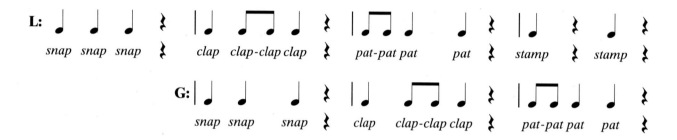

SECTION III:
THE LINGUISTIC INTELLIGENCE

Language and music share much in common. Both enter through the ear (and symbolically through the eye), are expressed through the mouth and hand, and are concerned with communication between people. This not only accounts for the ancient connection between poetry, music, and song, but also for Orff's intuition that speech is a child-sized bridge into music. Describing Orff's own music, Werner Thomas writes "(His music) originates always from within speech, giving freedom to the 'poetic idea.'"

My adapted definition of the linguistic intelligence includes:
- The capacity to perceive the verbal world accurately; hear the "music" of language.
- The capacity to hear, imitate, transform and to create meaning, syntax, and form.
- The capacity to hear, imitate, transform and to create nuances of verbal expression through imagery, story, and ideas.

A poet skilled in all of the above may experience the world like this:

> *I wanted to write poetry in the beginning because I had fallen in love with words. The first poems I knew were nursery rhymes, and before I could read them for myself, I had come to love just the words of them, the words alone. What the words stood for, symbolized, or meant, was of very secondary importance. What mattered was the sound of them. These words were, to me, as the notes of bells, the sounds of musical instruments, the noises of wind, sea, and rain, the rattle of milkcarts, the clopping of hooves on cobbles, the fingering of branches on a window pane. I cared for the shapes of sound that their names made in my ears, I cared for the colors the words cast on my eyes. I fell in love.*

—Dylan Thomas

People adept at language gravitate toward poetry, storytelling, theatre, fiction and nonfiction writing, public speaking, and courtroom law.

The use of speech, rhymes, and poetry as an inroad to music is one of the key characteristics of the Schulwerk. Using words to teach rhythm, rhymes to create melodies and instrumental arrangements, and poetry and story to inspire an integrated performance combining all the mediums, is common fare for the Orff teacher. The young child plays with the music of language and the language of music.

Name Games and *A Rhyme in Time,* published by Warner Bros. Publications, are two of my books that deal more extensively with the language/music connection. All of the activities in those books are easily adaptable to the percussion circle. I include a few similar activities in this collection, but mostly focus on rhymes and speech specifically related to percussion. The examples should give the novice Orff teacher a taste of this process and the seasoned Orff teacher some new accents.

14. NAME RHYTHMS

Focus: Linguistic Intelligence

Concept: Rhythm of words
         Changing timbres

Activity:

- Each person plays rhythm of name four times in turn around the circle; group echoes (make sure to pay attention to accent—Justine is different from Kevin, Sophia from Christopher, the first in each example beginning *before* the beat).

| Jus - tine, | Kev - in, | So - phi - a, | Chris - to - pher |

- As above, three times per name; two times; once.
- First person speaks and plays name four times, next joins in while first keeps playing. Continue adding names like this every two beats until all names in the circle are being spoken and played.

Jake	Jake	Jake	Jake	Jake	Jake	Jake	Jake	Jake	Jake
		Joan	Joan	Joan	Joan	Joan	Joan	Joan	Joan
				Geri	Geri	Geri	Geri	Geri	Geri
						Joey	Joey	Joey	Joey

- When leader calls "switch," all change to the name rhythm of the person to their right.
- Continue switching every eight beats. When everyone's name is "returned" to him or her, stop.
- As above without speaking—just clapping the rhythm of each name.

Variations:

- Each person plays own name seven times, then passes instrument to the left. Play own name again on the new instrument.
- During the opening echo activity, only those with instruments similar to the one being played play the echo.

Music extension:

Notate the different name rhythms and show score on board or paper.

Classroom application:

- Determine syllables by saying and clapping.
- Note use of accent in rhymes and poetry. For example, compare "**Doc**tor Foster went to Gloucester" that begins on the beat with "As **I** was going to St. Ives" that begins before it.

Comments:

This is yet another example of musical teaching: turning a necessary procedure of any class (learning names) into a musical event itself. Name games are an important part of our music education repertoire because:

- Teachers must know children's names for effective class process.
- Children need to know one another's names.
- All students want to feel known in class (even shy ones who seem to prefer to hide), and names are the first step.
- The variety of names, with their different syllables, accents, and sounds, create an automatic palette for colorful and contrasting orchestration.
- Basic musical concepts: beat (Dave), division of beat (Ashley), subdivision of beat (Annabella), accent (Suzanne), legato (Maria), staccato (Chuck), and more are all prepared through exploration of names.
- Our names are close to us, personal, immediate, helping create an atmosphere of intimacy and warmth.
- By beginning with something known—our names—and proceeding toward the unknown—their musical potential—we follow the grain of effective learning.

This game highlights orchestral texture through two distinct strategies. The first—paying attention to your neighbor's name rhythm while playing your own—requires the same kind of high attention skills practiced in Game 13: Simultaneous Canon. As each name is played on different instruments, the orchestration changes effortlessly without losing the flow. This game has the advantage of saying and internalizing everyone else's name and the excitement of discovering your own "returned" back to you.

The second strategy—keeping one's own name rhythm, but passing the instruments—achieves the same orchestral effect, but is easier to perform. You don't get to practice saying and playing everyone else's name, but you do get to try out each instrument in a short amount of time and hear how your own rhythm can sound so different.

15. NAMES OF INSTRUMENTS

Focus: Linguistic Intelligence

Concept: Rhythm of words
Onomatopoeia

Activity:
- Name each instrument in the circle until students know the name of each instrument.
- Each instrument plays the rhythm of its own name: drum ♩, woodblock ♩ ♩, triangle ♪♪♩ , finger cymbals ♪♪♪♪. Play one at a time around the circle (or one group at a time).
- As above, adding rhythms as in the previous name game.

Variations:
As above, creating different sounds on instrument for each syllable.

Music extension:
- Make a list of instruments with onomatopoetic names: reco-reco, angklung, cuica, dumbek, agung, tom-tom, etc.
- Research other categories of naming instruments: material (steel drum, log drum), shape (triangle, cuadro), technique (hand drum, vibraslap), tone description (flexatone, bull-roarer), inventor (waterphone, saxophone).

Classroom application:
- Have children create names for instruments based on sounds (the clanger, the dinger, the swoosher, etc.)
- Study the use of onomatopoeia in poetry. Mary O'Neill's poem "Feelings About Words" in Jack Prelutsky's collection *The Random House Book of Poetry for Children,* p. 197, is a wonderful introduction for children to the music of words.
- Create a verbal grouping of percussion instruments by first sounds, as in:

    Taiko, tabla, timpani, tom-tom,
    Steel drum, snare drum, slit drum, side drum,
    Bass drum, bongo drum, bombo, bodhran,
    Conga, cowbell, clave, gong.

Comments:
In the previous lessons, the children have explored the sound and compositional potential of the percussion instruments without having to know much about them. In the same way that children who have just met sometimes play with each other for a while without knowing each other's names, so might it be possible to go several classes without having named the instruments. If things have gone well, there is now a context for learning about them.

This game offers a musical approach to learning the names of the instruments. Naming anything brings it to a new level of reality for the young child, completing a structure of knowledge. The thing that has been seen, touched, heard (and often smelled and tasted as well!) now has a means for recall, as a single word triggers its memory in the imagination. Naming the instrument immediately confers a family (the Shaker family), a personality (it likes to be shaken) and eventually a first name to distinguish it from siblings and cousins—Ms. Maraca Shaker, Mr. Ganza Shaker, Miss Cabasa Shaker. This exercise integrates the content of the class (naming instruments) with the process (playing instruments) by using the names of the instruments as the springboard for group composition. The rhythm is the starting point, but we also use syllables to create different timbres and listen for onomatopoetic names.

16. NURSERY RHYME—BOW-WOW

Focus: Linguistic Intelligence

Concept: Speech rhythm
  Call-and-response

Bow-bow, *says the dog.* **Mew, mew,** *says the cat.*
Grunt, grunt, *goes the hog. And* **squeak** *goes the rat.*
Tu-whu, *says the owl,* **Caw, caw,** *says the crow.*
Quack, quack, *says the duck, And what the cuckoo says you know.* **Cuckoo.**

Activity:
- Recite text (you may wish to use visuals—words or pictures), pausing at the end and singing *Cuckoo* in the classic sol-mi falling interval. Encourage vocal qualities on the animal sounds that mimic the animal (high-pitched sung *tu-whu,* nasal *quack,* and so on).
- All play the underlined words as they appear in the text, speaking the rest.
- Reverse (speak underlined words, play the rest).
- Taking turns around the circle, each instrument plays one of the underlined parts. The remaining instruments play the rest.
- Make groups of seven, each group choosing seven instruments that aim to match the sonorities of each animal. Perform. (Double up instruments when groups are smaller than seven.)

Variations:
Explore movements of animals and use resulting percussion piece to accompany movement, i.e., half the group plays, the other half moves.

Music extension:
- Listen to music that incorporates animal sounds: Saint-Saëns' *The Carnival of the Animals,* Haydn's Symphony No. 83 ("The Hen"), Beethoven's Symphony No. 6 ("The Pastoral"), and so on.
- Collect, listen to, or sing the vast repertoire of pieces that include the cuckoo bird.

Classroom application:
Study the communication skills of animals.

Comments:

From the single spoken word of our name to the chanted grouping of words (as in names of instruments), we spiral out to the full-blown poem, with the whole of Mother Goose at our fingertips. The use of nursery rhymes to create both rhythmic and melodic pieces is standard practice in Orff-Schulwerk. My book, *A Rhyme in Time,* by Warner Bros. Publications, provides a larger collection of rhymes that are happily adaptable to this kind of work with percussion ensemble. For melodic/harmonic rhyme-based compositions, the five volumes of *Music for Children* (ed. Margaret Murray, pub. Schott) by Carl Orff and Gunild Keetman remains the source material.

I selected a nursery rhyme that used percussive words in a similar way to the following examples from other cultures. It is notable that they are virtually nonexistent in Mother Goose, though this is not surprising in light of the relative unimportance of the drum in the English folk tradition. Irish songs, with their nonsense refrains like "filla may oree oree ay," "whack fol the toor a loor a laddy," and "deedle diddle dum," offer a larger vocal percussive palette, echoing the use of the bodhran drum. The one given here suggests the form of featuring one instrument and offers the challenge of finding timbres close to animal sounds—a ratchet for the hog's grunt, a two-toned whistle for the owl, a baby's squeeze toy for the rat's squeak. The call-and-response form of soloist and group gives a satisfying texture, enough repetition for success and enough variety (the rat's phrase) for delicious contrast.

This is a good choice for the younger children—simple, playable, interesting to them (they love animals!), and effective.

17. PERCUSSIVE POEMS—GATA TUMBA

Focus: Linguistic Intelligence

Concept: Orchestration
Percussive tone color

Activity:

- Say the following text:

Gata tumba tumba tumba, con panderos y sonajas.	(with drums and jingle sticks)
Gata tumba tumba tumba, no te metas en las paja.	(don't step on the straw)
Gata tumba tumba tumba, toca el pito y el rabel,	(play the whistle and rebec)
Gata tumba tumba tumba, tamboril y cascabel.	(small drum and jingle bell)

- Group instruments by bass drum, hand drums, jingle bells, jingle stick, or tambourine, and whistles.
- Say each phrase and named instruments, repeating rhythm of last part of phrase. (Drums and jingle sticks play the rhythm "con panderos y sonajas" after first line is spoken. Since no instruments are mentioned in the second line, whole group clicks tongue to the rhythm in a warning, disapproving sound.)
- Bass drum plays "gata tumba tumba tumba," hitting edge of drum for "gata" and middle of skin for "tumba." Play whole text with bass drum followed by named instruments.

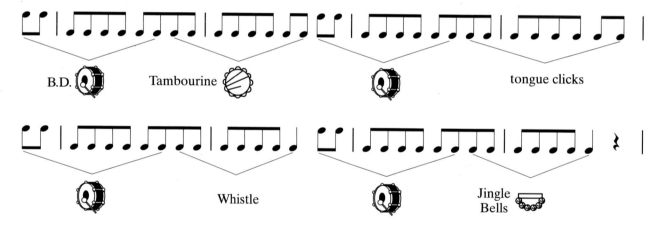

- Put into form: Say once, playing instruments. Play song on instruments. Sing song with all instruments playing the beat.

Variations:

- Play while marching in a processional.
- Compare or combine with other winter holiday songs mentioning percussion: "Jingle Bells," "Silver Bells," "The Little Drummer Boy," "The 12 Days of Christmas," and "Pat-a-Pan."

Music extension:

Listen to Sly and the Family Stone's song, "Dance to the Music," in which each instrument is introduced in the music and then plays a short solo.

Classroom application:

Investigate Spanish Christmas traditions.

Comments:

This festive Christmas song is about visiting the crib of the baby Jesus (hence, the admonition, don't step on the straw) with the celebratory feeling accented by the percussion instruments. In "Bow-Wow," the children had to decide which instruments should play. Here the text itself dictates who plays and when. This game also introduces the idea of two contrasting tones on one instrument as suggested by the contrast in "gata" and "tumba" in the text.

This, like many Spanish rhymes, is traditionally sung rather than chanted, as shown below.

Ga - ta tum - ba tum - ba, tum - ba con pan - de - ros y so - na - jas. Ga - ta tum - ba tum - ba tum - ba, no te me - tas en la pa - ja. Ga - ta tum - ba tum - ba tum - ba, to - ca_el pi - to_y el ra - bel. Ga - ta tum - ba tum - ba tum - ba, tam - bo - ril y cas - ca - bel.

18. PERCUSSIVE POEMS—SON MACARON TWO

Focus: Linguistic Intelligence

Concept: Percussive text
Group texture

Activity:

- Review previous "Son Macaron" activities on page 13.
- Each person chooses one of the following phrases to play: *tip tip tip; tap tap tap; one two three; beat beat beat; catch!* Students should try to match the timbre of the instrument with text. All sing and play chosen phrase when it appears in the song.
- As above, without singing (just thinking the words); again, with eyes closed.
- Decide on how to group the above, as in: triangles—*tip tip tip*; woodblocks—*tap tap tap*; drums—*one two three*; cowbells—*beat beat beat*; slapstick—*catch!*
- Above groupings play as ostinati throughout song:

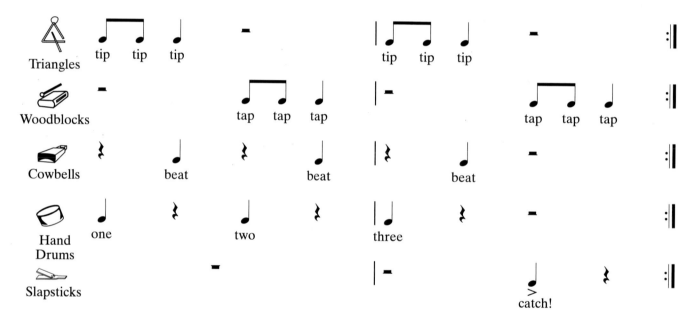

Variations:

- Divide first part of text hocket-style: *Son macaron, Son ferion, Marion marion, Leah leah.* Combine with second part and play whole song in order, each instrument group a different fragment of text.
- Change orchestration by having instruments switch parts.

Music extension:

Find examples of different orchestrations of the same tunes (I have recordings of a saxophone quartet, accordion duet and balalaika trio playing the same Bach piece!) and ask the children to compare and contrast.

Classroom application:

Play above parts on their desks or tables: a pencil on the table for *tip*; on a book for *tap*; opening and closing a book on *one beat, two beat, three beat*; closing a book forcefully on *catch!*

Comments:

By revisiting a song/game we've already played twice, the children receive yet another example of the immense possibilities of expanding any given material when the imagination is put to work. Using the words of the text to suggest particular instruments tunes the ear towards timbre and suggests that one of the demands of developing musical intelligence is to orchestrate with more careful attention. Attending to the vowel sounds, it is clear that *tip* should be higher pitched than *tap,* just as *tick* is higher than *tock.*

The second principle explored here is extracting patterns from the text and using them as repeated patterns throughout the song (such patterns are called "ostinato," or "ostinati," plural, and will be referred to as such in subsequent activities). This is yet another structure to build the aspect of musical intelligence that requires keeping one's part in multiple textures, again, aided here by language.

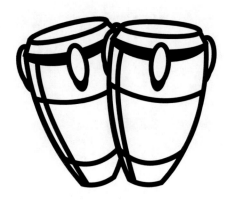

19. PERCUSSIVE POEMS—DEBAJO DE UN BOTÓN

Focus: Linguistic Intelligence

Concept: Percussive tone color
Complementary ostinati

Activity:
- Say the following text:

Debajo de un botón, ton, ton,	(Underneath a button)
del Señor Martín, tin, tin,	(Of Mr. Martin)
Había un ratón, ton, ton,	(There was a rat)
Ay qué chiquitín, tin, tin.	(Oh, how small!)

- All find two tones on instruments, one for *tin* and one for *ton*. Say or sing rhyme, playing the two sounds as they appear in the text.
- As above, thinking text only.
- Play *tin, tin, tin* and *ton, ton, ton* as an ostinato, shifting the accent to the final *tin* or *ton* of each group.

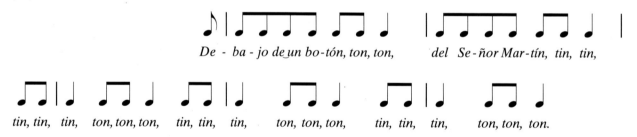

- Recite text while playing ostinati.

Variations:
- One half plays and/or recites the ostinato, the other half plays and/or recites the whole text.
- Compare with similar English rhymes:

  Miss Mary Mack, Mack, Mack
  All dressed in black, black, black,
  With silver buttons, buttons, buttons,
  All down her back, back, back.

- Follow the above activity sequence with "Miss Mary Mack."

De - ba - jo de_un bo - tón, ton, ton. Del Se - ñor Mar - tín, tin, tin, tin,

Ha - bía un ra - tón, ton, ton. Ay que chi - qui - tín, tin, tin.

Comments:

This game is similar to "Son Macaron," but instead of one instrument playing the higher-pitched word and other the lower, *each* instrument has to find a higher- and lower-pitched sound. This is easy for the double bell or bongo drum, but trickier for the triangle or single woodblock. Exploring sounds near the edge of the instrument and techniques of damping are some solutions. (Another is simply to do this class with two-toned percussion instruments!)

Playing the percussive sounds of the text as they appear is a simple beginning way to evoke rhythm. Internalizing the text and playing the rhythms alone is a much-used next step. Here the idea of displacing the rhythm for the text to use as a complementary ostinato is introduced—a higher level of musical thinking and skill. If it is too difficult to say and play at once for a particular child or group of children, have half the group play and the other half say (or play—see the first variation) the text.

20. PERCUSSIVE POEMS—OKINO TAIKO

Focus: Linguistic Intelligence

Concept: Drum language
          Instrument family

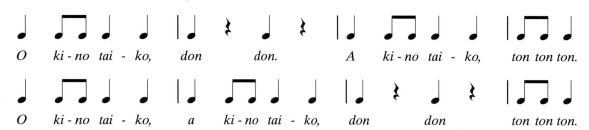

O   ki - no tai - ko,   don   don.   A   ki - no tai - ko,   ton ton ton.

O   ki - no tai - ko,   a   ki - no tai - ko,   don   don   ton ton ton.

Translation: Large taiko drum—*don don.* Small taiko drum—*ton ton ton.*

Activity:
- Set out percussion instruments in pairs—one bigger (group one), one smaller (group two).
- Recite above text and explain meaning. Invite the children to suggest how it should be played. If it's similar to the following sequence, try it. If it's different, try it.
- Larger instruments play on *don don,* smaller on *ton ton ton.*
- Group one only recites *okino taiko* and plays *don don.* Group two, the opposite (plays *okino taiko* and recited *don don*).
- Create with partner a short piece combining the *dons* and *tons* of the two instruments. When performing, each speaks piece first and then plays.

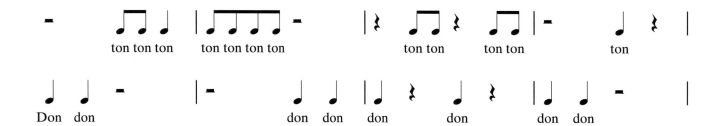

ton ton ton   ton ton ton ton   ton ton   ton ton   ton

Don don   don don don   don   don don

Variations:
- Each person plays composed piece on two instruments.
- Learn more taiko drum language, as in the phrase:

Don   don   don, ka - ra ka ka, don don   don don, ka - ra - ka ka.

The *karaka's* hit on the edge of the drum for a wood sound. Create new patterns.

Music extension:
- Study about taiko drums through live performance (check your local community, videos, recordings, and books).
- Starting with the school collection, discuss the concept of family. A conga and djembe might be thought of as cousins, whereas three congas of different sizes are brothers and sisters (or parents and children). Find photos and recorded examples of other such musical families playing together.

Classroom application:
- Extend the instrument/family metaphor to an imaginative story about one's own family. How is the power and beauty of the small drum different from that of the big? What does each have to contribute?
- Use the above poem and taiko drum research in a Japanese culture study.

Comments:

It has been said many times that Orff's use of speech to release rhythm is a universal practice. This exercise is an excellent example, introducing both the names of drums from Japan and one of the speech syllables used to teach pieces in this tradition. Taiko drumming is a new incarnation of an old art form that originated on Sado Island off the coast of Japan. Since the 1960s, many ensembles in Japan and elsewhere have formed. There is a thriving Taiko community in San Francisco, and several of my students take Taiko classes. A typical ensemble includes many different size drums, woodblocks, bamboo flutes, brass bells, conch shells, and more. The drumming is powerful and the technique highly stylized and dance-like—the manner of striking the drums and the choreography of drummers moving between drums is an integral part of the art form.

This little poem is a lovely example of a self-teaching piece, with all the information embedded in the text. Like Montessori materials, the teacher is not needed to create an interesting lesson—the children can figure it out and probably come up with more interesting variations as well. Keep in mind that this is the spirit of *all* these games.

Though the primary focus here is once again the use of language to transmit both the rhythms and the form of a piece, the study of larger and smaller is an equally potent use of the poem. Understanding relationships between little and high, big and low, is not only an essential introduction to the SATB nature of much music, but a large component of xylophone playing (high C is smaller than low C). Invariably, the child may notice a smaller drum with a lower pitch than a bigger one and here the concept of tightness and tension in skins and strings comes up.

21. MIDDLE EASTERN DRUM LANGUAGE

Focus: Linguistic Intelligence

Concept: Additive rhythms

Activity:
This activity works best with a circle of drums, preferably those that can be played by hand (dumbeks, frame drums, congas, djembes, and so on). Using a soft mallet in the center of a drum and a stick for the edge can also work.

- Explore techniques for getting an open, resonant sound in or near the center of the drum and name it *dum* (pronounced "doom"). Explore ways to get a higher pitched, short, sharp sound on the edge of the drum and name it *tak* (pronounced "tock") (*taka* can be used for eighth notes).

- Vocally echo patterns based on *dum* and *tak,* and then play on drum.

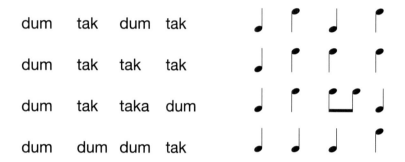

- Repeat above exercise with partners, one   leading echo, the other following. Switch.
- Each person creates a four- or eight-beat pattern of *dum*s, *tak*s, and *taka*s. Share one at a time around circle.
- All learn first person's pattern. All learn second's. Join the two together, repeating each twice.

Together: dum dum tak tak / dum dum tak tak /
             dum-dum dum-tak tak / dum-dum dum-tak tak

- Continue as above, adding third person's pattern and then the fourth person's.
- Following above model, groups of four create their own pieces. This time, first person alone makes up pattern, second person listens carefully and decides how to relate his or her pattern (repeat beginning part of it and change ending, or change beginning and keep ending, etc.). The group may choose to repeat one person's pattern before going to the next.

- Perform.

Variations:
- Build an extended piece combining the ideas of each small group.
- Learn a classic Middle Eastern rhythm, like the Egyptian *baladi*.

Dum Dum   Tak Dum   Tak

- Add rhythms within basic pattern:

D D   T D   T T
D D   T D   t t T

Music extension:
- Study and listen to examples of Middle Eastern drumming.
- Listen to new music inspired by Middle Eastern percussion and percussion techniques: "Ramana" from *Music of the World,* Glen Velez; CDH-307.

Classroom application:
Build a cumulative story, one phrase per person, each person adding to the phrase before:
1. *Bob and Betty went to the store.*
2. *Bob and Betty went to the store and they bought some bread.*
3. *Bob and Betty went to the store and they bought some bread. The bread had mold on it.*
4. *Bob and Betty went to the store and they bought some bread. The bread had mold on it. The mold grew and spread over the entire house.*
5. *Bob and Betty went to the store and they bought some bread. The bread had mold on it. The mold grew and spread over the entire house. The house crumbled.*
6. *Bob and Betty went to the store and they bought some bread. The bread had mold on it. The mold grew and spread over the entire house. The house crumbled. When the house crumbled, Bob and Betty needed to buy a new one.*
7. *Bob and Betty went to the store and they bought some bread. The bread had mold on it. The mold grew and spread over the entire house. The house crumbled. When the house crumbled, Bob and Betty needed to buy a new one. Bob and Betty went to the store.*

Comments:
Here we can get a feeling for how our multiple approaches to rhythm begin to build on one another. The matching of tone and color in percussive poems (games 17–19) is reversed: Instead of matching instrument sounds to the given words, speech is created to match the instrumental tone. (Many theorize that this was the origin of scat singing in jazz—an attempt to duplicate the articulations of trumpets and saxophones in the voice.) It calls for a precise kinesthetic technique to achieve a precise aural effect.

This exercise also introduces an additive concept of rhythmic composition, joining small rhythmic cells to create a larger compositional body. The approach of group composition, each student contributing an idea that is taken up by the others, hits both the intrapersonal dimension—expression through creation—and an interpersonal one, offering composition up to group creation. At the end of the process, the piece belongs to everyone, for each has contributed equally to the final result. You may well understand my excitement in first reading Gardner's Theory of Multiple Intelligences and discovering how it described the ways Orff teachers have been working for more than fifty years!

It should be clear that we have now entered the stage of precision. An activity like this should follow the initial, more exploratory structures. Once the children's curiosity about and comfort with the percussion instruments has been awakened, they are hungry to know more about precise techniques, procedures, concepts, and other means to control and extend their expression. At the same time, the invitation to create keeps the unknown sufficiently in the picture to keep the inquisitive mind and listening ear alert and healthy.

These syllables come from the Middle Eastern tradition of frame drums, tambourines, and goblet drums, many of which have different names across national borders—the tar (frame drum), the riq (tambourine), and the dumbek or darrabuka (goblet drum), to name just a few. Each naturally has preferred playing techniques.

SECTION IV:
THE LOGICAL-MATHEMATICAL INTELLIGENCE

Though it is tempting to make one-to-one correspondences between intelligences and school subjects, i.e., linguistic = language arts; logical-mathematical = math; kinesthetic = physical education; visual-spatial = art; musical = music; interpersonal = recess; and so on, each subject calls on every intelligence for full comprehension. We have had a taste of how important language is to music-making and music-learning. Here we will explore some of the deep structures of logic and math inherent in music and discover how to enter music through them to increase understanding, compositional thinking, and expressive playing. Some of the characteristics of the logical-mathematical intelligence include:
- The capacity to perceive the beauty of numbers.
- The capacity to perceive, transform, and create patterns and relationships.
- The capacity to perceive cause-and-effect and to perform concrete operations to achieve measurable results.
- The capacity to draw inferences, develop theories, and prove hypotheses.

Someone who tuned into the wavelength of this intelligence might be described as follows:

> *At the height of Isaac Newton's powers there was in him a compelling desire to find order and design in what appeared to be chaos, to distill from a vast inchoate mass of materials a few basic principles that would embrace the whole and define the relationships of its component parts.... in whatever direction he turned, he was searching for a unifying structure.*
>
> —Frank Manuel

People tuned in to this intelligence tend to gravitate to mathematics, engineering, various sciences, computers, car repair, grammar, music theory, and accounting.

Pattern is so essential to composition that one might say music is sounded pattern, math made audible. Virtually every aspect of music is described mathematically: quarter notes, 3/4 meter, 86 on the metronome, A=440 cycles per second, minor third, I chord with a flatted seventh, 60 decibels, binary structure. From rhythm to pitch to form, the link between the logical-mathematical intelligence and music study is clear. (Some have speculated that a large part of the computer industry was built by out-of-work musicians!)

The best way to begin to learn math is to play with objects. The brain's natural inclination to reveal pattern and create order sets the young blockbuilder sorting and arranging. Formal math study requires that foundation and proceeds to name the patterns, develop operations, and reveal functions, moving toward higher levels of abstractions. Likewise, the best way to learn music is to play it and play with it, noticing patterns and relationships. Formal music study names the patterns (division of the beat is called eighth notes, beats grouped in four generally 4/4 meter), develop operations (start the same pattern at a different time to create canon), and reveal functions (the V7 chord is leaning toward the I chord and falls into resolution), thus moving the intuitive discoveries of musical play toward the rules of musical grammar.

The difference between math study and musical theory is small, but significant. In math, the theory either serves the practical use of balancing checkbooks and building bridges or shines with the luster of its own self-reflected abstraction. In music, the theory must always be subservient to the aesthetic effect. Though there are those who revel in the sheer beauty of music theory on paper and can spend hours discussing the upper partials of the overtone series, the math of music serves to increase our ability to understand, create and perform music that tickles the ear and feeds the soul.

The exercises in this section serve the playful aspect of developing the logical-mathematical intelligence, building the foundation for both the theory particular to music study and the ordered thinking central to the math class. They touch on the body of knowledge that characterizes traditional music study, but enter through a playful approach, building a context for further investigation. Watch the children carefully to determine their level of interest in pursuing the concepts. If they seem excited by the ideas, it means that they're ready for them. If they seem bored, it's because they're not yet ready—more play is needed. Follow their lead while simultaneously leading them toward an understanding that they can follow.

22. FOUR-LEVEL CANON

Focus: Logical-Mathematical Intelligence

Concept: Duration values (division)
    Diminution

Activity:

- Teach the following pattern in body percussion:

- Repeat as above, four beats at each level:

- Repeat as above, two beats at each level:

- Perform four-beat pattern as canon:

- Perform two-beat pattern as canon:

- Perform two-beat canon entering after one beat:

Variations:

- Instead of each person performing snaps, claps, pats, and stamps, divide into four groups around the circle, one for each level. (Snap group perform four beats followed by clap, etc.)
- Transfer above to four percussion groups: finger cymbals = snap; frame drum = clap; conga drums = pat; bass drums = stamp.
- Add text, as in: *Apple, pear, pomegranate, plum.*
- Each instrument group plays all four levels (snap, clap, pat, stamp) in canon.

Music extension:

- Write out the entire piece in traditional notation.
- Listen to recordings of Javanese gamelan music in which all four durations (and more) are played simultaneously by the different instrumental groupings in the orchestra.

Classroom application:

Have the students summarize the mathematical operations involved—division of beat into eighth and sixteenth notes; elongation in half notes; total number of beats per phrase in a four-beat pattern (16), in a two-beat pattern (8), in a one-beat pattern (4); totals counting repetitions of phrases—16 x 2, 8 x 4, 4 x 8, and so on. Have them create their own graphic notation to summarize the piece.

Comments:

This little piece is one of my favorite ways to begin workshops. Without a word spoken, I begin snapping and the group joins in. They follow as I change to clapping, then patting, then stamping, and return to snapping. The next time through, I play eight beats at each level, with the group still following. After several times through, confident in the brain's need to perceive pattern, I stop and indicate for the group to go on to see if they have it. Once it's clear that they know it, I give a signal to stop, gesture to create four different groups in the circle, and begin the pattern again with group one. After eight beats, I nod to group two to enter, and so on, until all four groups are playing in canon. While they play, I stand in the center, pointing out how the claps travel around (or the pats, snaps, stamps). When it feels right, I gesture in turn for each group to stop, immediately indicate to group one a shorter pattern, and without losing a beat, they begin with four beats per level, each group coming in accordingly. Following the same procedure, we reduce to two beats and finally, two beats again, but with each group entering one beat later. When I stop each group, there is a dramatic silence and then a murmur of appreciation. We have created a little piece in the space of five to ten minutes with great energy and excitement—all without a word being spoken!

We also have effortlessly introduced key concepts and experiences that set both the tone of the class and provide a foundation for the lessons to come. Among them:

- Our body percussion instruments—snap, clap, pat, stamp.
- Duration values—half, quarter, eighth and sixteenth notes.
- The importance of the circle for focus and visual effect (seeing, as well as hearing, the rhythms traveling around).
- Canon.
- Nonverbal communication.
- Transforming musical exercise to musical piece, through clear beginning, a middle that changes and develops, an unbroken flow, and a clear ending.
- The group nature of the work.

This is also a good demonstration of the ways body percussion can lead to percussion instruments. The snaps mirror the technique of finger cymbals; the claps of frame drums (sometimes called hand drums); the pats of conga drums; and the stamps of the bass drum of the trap set played with a pedal. (If unavailable, bass drum played with a mallet is acceptable.) These instruments also come close to the timbres of the above body percussion.

The sequence I describe at the beginning of these comments emphasizes canon, but the activity itself is adapted to suit percussion instruments, i.e., each instrumental group only plays one part of the canon in the sequence given (though canon is suggested in the variations). This piece is possible to extend to the xylophones as well.

This exercise also amply demonstrates why children who study music extensively tend to do well in math—they are constantly immersed in a world of additions, subtractions, multiplications, and divisions. This is not to naively suggest that simply playing music will increase math scores. It clearly does provide the experiential foundation for future understanding, but experience alone cannot make the important leap to cognitive awareness. That requires reflection, analysis, and the naming of concepts and procedures. Every time we take a moment of the music class to discuss the patterns we have performed or created, we are further feeding the logical-mathematical intelligence.

Yet better math scores are not our purpose—we should only spend as much time as we need in theory before turning back to our aesthetic and expressive goals. The ideal partnership involves the classroom teacher extending these activities with Cuisenaire rods and beads, graph paper, and math worksheets.

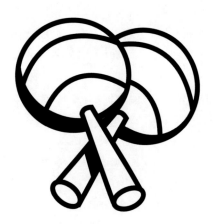

23. POETIC STRUCTURE

Focus: Logical-Mathematical Intelligence

Concept: Binary and tripartite form

Activity:
- Begin the class in a circle with no instruments. Recite the following rhymes with the children.

Skip, skip, skip to my lou,
Skip, skip, skip to my lou,
Skip, skip, skip to my lou,
Skip to my lou my darling.
(a a a b)

Humpty Dumpty sat on the wall.
Humpty Dumpty had a great fall.
All the king's horses and all the king's men,
Couldn't put Humpty together again.
(a a b b)

Come butter come,
Come butter come.
Peter's standing at the gate,
Waiting for his butter cake.
Come butter come.
(a a b b a)

Pease porridge hot,
Pease porridge cold,
Pease porridge in the pot,
Nine days old.
(a a b c)

Hickety pickety, my black hen.
She lays eggs for gentlemen.
Sometimes nine and sometimes ten.
Hickety pickety, my black hen.
(a b b a)

Hickory dickory dock,
The mouse ran up the clock.
The clock struck one, the mouse ran down.
Hickory dickory dock.
(a b c a)

- All clap the rhythm of rhymes while saying them. Without saying them.
- All clap the first two phrases of a rhyme. If second phrase is different, change to pat.
- Follow the form of the poem by playing the rhythm with claps, pats, and snaps.
- Have the children write on the board or on paper an outline of each poem's form (given above) using "a b c" to represent rhythmic phrases. (Note: If two phrases share the same rhythm, but have different words, they are still labeled as "a a.")
- Have children form groups of four around the circle, choose a poem, and pick instruments to match the form (as in "shaker shaker guiro ratchet" for "a a b c").
- Each plays rhythm of text in order (i.e., first shaker plays *Pease porridge hot,* second *Pease porridge cold,* guiro *Pease porridge in the pot,* ratchet *Nine days old.*)
- First person in each group makes up a four- or eight-beat rhythm. The second either echoes (if form begins "a a") or makes up an answer (if form is "a b"). Continue following whole form. (Thus, "a b b a" would be "statement, answer, echo the answer, echo the statement.")
- At the end of each four-person performance (*Come butter come* may have five people), the whole group repeats back the entire composed piece.

Variations:

Above exercise without instruments matching form.

Music extension:

Listen to and analyze the rhythmic structure of famous melodies that follow these forms:*

- "Six Variations on a Swiss Song," Beethoven—a a b a
- "Strange Lands and People," Schumann, and "I Got Rhythm," Gershwin—a a a b
- "Musette," Bach—a a b c
- "Hallelujah Chorus," Handel—a a b b c
- "Melody," Schumann—a b a b
- "Ecossaise in G," Beethoven—a a b b

Classroom application:

Analyze other rhymes and poems as above.

Comments:

This lesson is a clear model of a vital process of development—moving from concrete to abstract and then back again to concrete at a higher level of skill and understanding. The familiar nursery rhyme is the starting point, the given known from which students head toward the unknown: the rhythmic form of the poems. Beginning with hands-on exploration of the form—the sequence that begins with clapping the rhythm of the words and concludes with changing from claps to pats—the students move toward a symbolic abstraction of the form, using letters to represent phrase structure. That abstraction again becomes more concrete as students choose three-dimensional instruments to demonstrate the form and then audibly concrete as they turn the abstraction back toward the making of music.

This alone is an impressive learning sequence, but the Orff-trained teacher doesn't stop there. He or she calls upon previous activities of echo and question/answer (familiar knowns), but now in a markedly different context (a novel unknown). The creative imagination again awakens, but instead of a freewheeling romp through the meadows of limitless possibility, it now must exercise within the small room of a precise structure. Here the child encounters one of the most intriguing mysteries of creation: that sometimes imposed structures limit and confine the musical imagination, and sometimes they fortify and invigorate it. Keeping in mind the musically expressive end of all our investigations, the group may discover that these echo and question/answer improvisations following these simple forms will be more musically satisfying than the open-ended ones explored earlier.*

I find it moving that the lifelong search for the balance of freedom and structure is present from the very beginning of a child's formal music study. The freedom minus the structure is a self-indulgent tangle and the structure minus the freedom is a lifeless shell. It is largely the logical-mathematical intelligence that reveals just how much form is necessary for coherent music.

---

* This is true of all music. Listen to a Charlie Parker saxophone solo and you'll hear a freedom that gives the sensation of unmediated spontaneous musical expression. Analyze a transcription of the same solo and you'll see slight variations on particular melodic patterns every time he arrives at certain chords in the structure.

24. SOUND ALLOWANCE

Focus: Logical-Mathematical Intelligence

Concept: Random pattern
         Space

Activity:
Give the group a "sound allowance." For example, students make five sounds on their instrument, and *they* decide when to play them, i.e., all five together; three in a row and later two more; one sound every 30 seconds, etc. When all five are played, the instrument is set down. When all instruments are down, the piece is over.

Variations:
Give a different allowance to each instrument group or person, i.e., triangle gets four, drum gets twelve, vibraslap gets one, and so on.

Music extension:
Listen to music with lots of space in it: "Five Pieces for Orchestra, Op. 10," Anton Webern, Count Basie's piano solo on "One O'Clock Jump."

Classroom application:
- Give students a "question allowance" for one day. Each may only ask five questions, but he or she decides when, must keep track of them, must spend the whole allowance before the day is over, but may not get an advance and ask more. Prepare or supplement with stories about genies and three wishes.
- Prepare lessons about filling space—compare Japanese haiku and English epic poetry; Hemingway and Dickens; Joan Miro's *Blue II* and Bosch's paintings; species diversity in an acre of rainforest and a desert, etc.

Comments:
The sound allowance is an image that helps create a sparse soundscape. It provides an upper limit that invites students to choose their moment carefully, listening for the right moment to enter. Whatever the musical result, personalities will definitely emerge—the spendthrifts, the hoarders, the ones who can't keep track—with implications for both financial futures and artistic styles.

25. COMING TOGETHER

Focus: Logical-Mathematical Intelligence

Concept: Polymeter
　　　　　Common denominator

Activity:
- In partners, each partner silently chooses a number from one to five. Both partners clap their chosen number at the same time to the same beat, leaving a one-beat rest at the end (For example, three would be cl. cl. cl. 𝄽 cl. cl. cl. 𝄽 etc.). Both partners need to listen—and look— for the moment they share a rest and then immediately change to a new number. If both choose the same number, they clap it three times and the piece is over. Here is a sample game:

	Note that partners did not choose the same number.			Note that partners chose the same number(s).	

cl.	cl.	cl.	𝄽	cl.	cl.	cl.	𝄽	cl.	cl.	cl.	𝄽	cl.	cl.	cl.	cl.	𝄽	cl.	cl.	cl.	cl.	𝄽	cl.	cl.	cl.	cl.	𝄽	cl.	cl.	cl.	cl.	cl.	𝄽	cl.	cl.	cl.	cl.	cl.	𝄽	cl.	cl.	cl.	cl.	cl.	𝄽
cl.	cl.	𝄽	cl.	cl.	𝄽	cl.	cl.	𝄽	cl.	cl.	𝄽	cl.	cl.	cl.	𝄽	cl.	cl.	cl.	𝄽	cl.	cl.	cl.	𝄽	cl.	cl.	cl.	𝄽	cl.	cl.	cl.	cl.	cl.	𝄽	cl.	cl.	cl.	cl.	cl.	𝄽	cl.	cl.	cl.	cl.	cl.	𝄽

- Transfer to percussion instruments.

Variations:
- Try with eyes closed—just listening.
- Reverse by internalizing the beat and playing the rest.
- Play in groups of three.
- Experiment with alike instruments (two cowbells pitched apart) and different instruments (bell and drum).
- Work out the math and play as a whole group composition (with five different groups).

1	𝄽	1	𝄽	1	𝄽	1	𝄽	1	𝄽	1	𝄽	1	𝄽	1	𝄽	1	𝄽	1	𝄽	1	𝄽	1	𝄽	1	𝄽	1	𝄽	1	𝄽	1	𝄽	1	𝄽	1	𝄽	1	𝄽	1	𝄽
1	2	𝄽	1	2	𝄽	1	2	𝄽	1	2	𝄽	1	2	𝄽	1	2	𝄽	1	2	𝄽	1	2	𝄽	1	2	𝄽	1	2	𝄽	1	2	𝄽	1	2	𝄽	1	2	𝄽	
1	2	3	𝄽	1	2	3	𝄽	1	2	3	𝄽	1	2	3	𝄽	1	2	3	𝄽	1	2	3	𝄽	1	2	3	𝄽	1	2	3	𝄽	1	2	3	𝄽	1	2		
1	2	3	4	𝄽	1	2	3	4	𝄽	1	2	3	4	𝄽	1	2	3	4	𝄽	1	2	3	4	𝄽	1	2	3	4	𝄽	1	2	3	4	𝄽	1	2			
1	2	3	4	5	𝄽	1	2	3	4	5	𝄽	1	2	3	4	5	𝄽	1	2	3	4	5	𝄽	1	2	3	4	5	𝄽	1	2	3	4	5	𝄽	1	2	3	4	5	𝄽

1	𝄽	1	𝄽	1	𝄽	1	𝄽	1	𝄽	1	𝄽	1	𝄽	1	𝄽					(1's - 30 times)
1	2	𝄽	1	2	𝄽	1	2	𝄽	1	2	𝄽	1	2	𝄽	1	2	𝄽	1	2	𝄽	(2's - 20 times)
3	𝄽	1	2	3	𝄽	1	2	3	𝄽	1	2	3	𝄽	1	2	3	𝄽			(3's - 15 times)
3	4	𝄽	1	2	3	4	𝄽	1	2	3	4	𝄽	1	2	3	4	𝄽			(4's - 12 times)
1	2	3	4	5	𝄽	1	2	3	4	5	𝄽	1	2	3	4	5	𝄽			(5's - 10 times)

Music extension:
Listen to Steve Reich's "Drumming" to hear a compositional extension of this idea.

Classroom application:

Graph with three-dimensional objects or on paper. Have the students work out the math. (In the above example, three plus the rest is four, two plus the rest is three, four and three share a common denominator of twelve—thus, the four will repeat three times and the three repeats four times before sharing a rest.)

Comments:

This is a game that came my way through the "street culture" of music teachers. Someone once said he heard it as an actual composition in a new-music festival. It's a fantastic partner-cooperation exercise and attentive-listening device. It's also good for parties, long waits at bus stops, and something the kids in the back seat can do in between wondering, "When are we gonna get there?"

SECTION V:
THE VISUAL-SPATIAL INTELLIGENCE

Though the visual-spatial intelligence is called forth most clearly in the visual arts, it is in the foreground of various branches of math and logic (geometry, chess); science (physics, engineering); sports (basketball, skiing); dance and drama (choreography, blocking); and daily life (driving, map-reading). It can be described as:

- The capacity to perceive the visual world accurately; transform and modify one's perceptions.
- The capacity to perceive the beauty in shapes and forms.
- The capacity to recreate imagery internally.
- The capacity to orient oneself in space.
- The capacity to estimate intervals of time and space.

A visually-spatially gifted person may experience the world like this:

> *The artist thinks of sculpture, whatever its size, as if he were holding it completely enclosed in the hollow of his hand; he mentally visualizes a complex form from all around itself. He knows while he looks at one side what the other side is like; he identifies himself with its center of gravity, its mass, its weight; he realizes its volume, as the space that the shape displaces in the air.*
>
> —Henry Moore

The visual aspect of music in the West is so strong that the notated score is called "the music." The tradition of playing music by decoding symbols calls more upon the visual, logical, and kinesthetic intelligences than the musical one—a rather odd approach that works fine for some and miserably for others (hence, the multidimensional approach offered in this book to attempt to reach all learning styles and preferences). The spatial aspect of music manifests in a variety of ways: the gamelan teacher playing the instrument upside down, the stride piano player reaching for the notes in the broken chords of the left hand, the singer aiming for the high note, and the composer getting a sense of the overall development of a piece are all using a spatial intelligence. In the Orff classroom rich in kinesthetic opportunities, the ability to move through space in the choreography of folk dance and creative movement is likewise a function of this intelligence.

The following activities are designed to playfully explore sounds and sound structures released by visual cues and activities.

26. CONDUCTOR

Focus: Visual-Spatial Intelligence

Concept: Sound from gesture

Activity:

Seated circle with percussion instruments grouped in sections. Conductor is in center: he or she starts and stops sounds with gestures. Some common signals: start, stop, continue playing, short sound, long sound, loud sound, soft sound. The conductor may make unmetered sounds, start patterns going and start other patterns to join in, and sweep around the circle, all improvised on the spot. Students must be attentive and translate all of the conductor's gestures to sound.

Variations:

- Two conductors simultaneously in the center, maintaining awareness of each other's music and sensing when to end.
- The conductor leads with eyes closed. (This idea came from a blind workshop participant who volunteered to conduct. She quickly got a sense of where the different instruments were, but at first there was a marvelous element of surprise.)

Music extension:

Watch a video of a symphonic conductor. Turn off the sound and imagine the music. Turn off the sound and *make* the music.

Classroom application:

- Give directions for an activity silently, gesturing all instructions.
- Have students tell a story through gesture and movement (mime).

Comments:

This is a simple structure that accomplishes much. It is an excellent free-form introduction to the art of conducting both from the standpoint of the child conducting and the group following. For the group, it helps hone a skill that is not automatic in all children (to put it mildly!)—keeping visually focused on a leader and responding to the leader's cues. For the music to work, each student must pay 100 percent attention, which reminds him or her of the responsibility to be fully present in the experience.

For the conductor, it is a marvelous experience of great power—a simple wave of the hand and a sound emerges! That sense of control and of immediate feedback from the environment is exciting for children, who often feel at the other end of other people's—parents, teachers, and adults in general—control. It can also be scary to be in charge. This hits both extremes of the personality spectrum: the confident, aggressive child who acts out in class is given an accepted form for that energy, and the shy, withdrawn child is a given a ritual space to come forth. (How often I've been amazed by "shy" children who step forth confidently and expressively in dramatic play!)

This is also an excellent opportunity for you as the teacher to observe each child as conductor. Though some children at first may appear to be simply waving arms around, in fact, the quality of their musical thinking becomes strikingly transparent, both visually and aurally. Because you are not needed to lead the exercise, you are free to take notes on the musical decisions of each conductor.

Some wonderful music emerges in this exercise. The variety of possibilities is surprising, and each conductor will offer a new idea.

27. INSTRUMENT SHAPE

Focus: Visual-Spatial Intelligence

Concept: Archetypal shapes

Activity:
- Create small groups of three to five people, each group with a chosen percussion instrument. Two or more duplicate the shape of the instrument in their bodies; if there is a mallet, one may also take the shape of the mallet. One person plays the actual instrument while the others mime that playing, including the effect of the striking on the vibration of the instrument.
- Decide on a clear, simple rhythm or choose a leader, i.e., the instrument player will play and the mimes follow, or reversed.

Variations:
Compose a percussion piece for two or more instruments with some playing and some miming. Consider a middle section in which the mimed "instruments" break apart and dance.

Music extension:
Classify the five most basic shapes found in instruments.

Classroom application:
- Name the most basic shapes of instruments: circles, squares, triangles, lines, pears, etc.
- Draw or paint a picture abstracting instrument shapes. Compare with Picasso's *Three Musicians; Accordionists; Guitar; Musical Instruments*; and Braque's *Still Life With Musical Instruments; The Clarinet, Guitar and Compote*.

Comments:
This is a rather strange idea that always produces hilarious results. It certainly is not the most obvious thing to do with percussion instruments, yet the ability to leap like this, from one mode (intelligence) to another, helps children keep their imagination intact. Both the leap and the humor invite divergent thinking. In a world in which the old answers to new dilemmas don't suffice, we need to train the next generation to imagine beyond the borders.

The ability to recreate the shape of an instrument in the body draws on our visual-spatial skills, but also on our kinesthetic intelligence—one of many examples of how these multiple intelligences never occur in isolation.

28. INSTRUMENT SCULPTURE

Focus: Visual-Spatial Intelligence

Concept: Three-dimensional group sculpture

Activity:
- In a circle, all play improvised or composed rhythms. One person stops playing and places his or her instrument in the center. One at a time, each person adds his or her instrument to the emerging sculpture. No one may change the placement of another's instrument, but must make a clear choice as to where to put his or her instrument in the overall design.
- At the end, all circle around the instruments to see the sculpture from all sides, striking poses of learned museum goers and making intelligent comments.
- Leave the instruments for the next class to see or take the instruments out in reverse order, one at a time, playing them once more.

Variations:
- Create other shapes and patterns on the floor—circles, lines, spirals. Decide on patterns (drum drum woodblock drum drum bell, etc.) and decide which lay flat or can stand up. (This will, of course, exercise our logical-mathematical intelligence!)
- Take photographs of the results, draw the final sculpture, or recreate it in the body (as in previous exercise).
- Take an existing percussion piece or create one and include instrument sculpture in the performance.
- Go into the school or neighborhood playground and "play" the climbing structures with sticks as a giant musical instrument sculpture.

Music extension:
Through video, books or visits, study new instruments fashioned in a sculptural way (e.g., The Harry Partch collection, Murray Shafer's barn in Menuhin's *Music of Man*).

Classroom application:
- Create a sculpture with classroom materials: pencils, rulers, papers, books, etc.
- Brainstorm ways in which the classroom might be more aesthetically arranged while still being practical.

Comments:
When children walk into a class in which the teacher has already artfully arranged the instruments or other materials, it sets a tone of mystery and expectation. It communicates that aesthetics matter by paying attention to how things are arranged in space. These exercises are the visual equivalents of sound improvisations, each student responding to another by complementing, accenting, and extending the previous choice of how to fill space. The group compositional process may lack the unified vision of the individual creation (and children will express their disappointment in other's choices!), but makes up for it in the excitement, give-and-take, and mystery of group creation.

29. GRAPHIC NOTATION

Focus: Visual/Spatial Intelligence

Concept: Symbol to sound

Activity:

- Each student draws a score using "graphic notation," an individualized indication of symbols representing sounds, with or without explanatory keys.
- Each student plays and shares his score.
- Partners exchange and play each other's scores.
- Select some and put them together to create a larger piece, playing them at the same time or one after another.

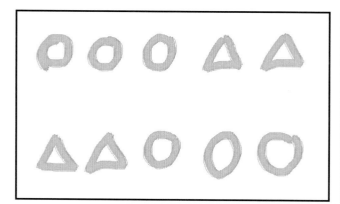 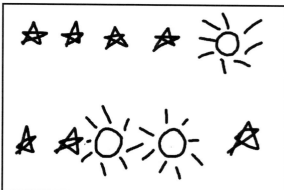

Variations:

- Reverse the above. Leader improvises music, and each student in the group simultaneously notates it graphically.
- Select pieces of modern art and play them as graphic notation scores: Piet Mondrian's *Composition in Blue B,* Bart Van der Leck's *Geometric Composition.*

Music extension:

- Look at examples of scores throughout the centuries, ranging from Gregorian chants to modern compositions.
- Look at examples of notational systems and scores from other cultures.

Classroom application:

- Redo the scores, using color, paint, or other materials and display.
- Make a graphic score representing the main characters and action of a story like *Goldilocks and the Three Bears.*

Comments:

This exercise serves as both a valid form of creating and preserving music, and is a playful entry into traditional music notation. It is "real" in itself, with its counterparts in professional scores, its exciting overlap between sight and sound, and its invitation to create some unique music. Its subjectivity and imprecision leave space for the performer to interpret, indeed, demands more involvement from the performer in deciphering the notation. At the same time, it highlights the need for more precision in tone and time, and for an objective standard understandable by all— hence, an excellent step to traditional notation.

As fun as these exercises are, it is important to keep in mind that there are limits to the possible interchanges between intelligences and the defining borders of each intelligence that are essential. The ear and the eye, serving as outposts of the musical and visual intelligences, have their own frame of reference. No great composition was created through trying to literally translate a visual idea. Likewise, no great piece of art was ever made following the contours of sound. Though much of this book accents the fluidity of borders, each discipline has its own techniques, vocabularies, unique principles, and creative demands, and each needs its own time and space to develop. There is wisdom in having special times and teachers for art, music, dance, and drama. Reducing it all to a generic integrated arts approach is a disservice to each field.

Vietnamese Temple Blocks

30. KINESTHETIC GRAPHIC NOTATION

Focus: Visual-Spatial Intelligence

Concept: Action to sound

Activity:
- Lay out a group of objects: scarves, balloons, balls, soap bubbles. Demonstrate possibilities of "conducting" with objects. Some examples:
  - Waving, throwing, juggling scarves; different instruments for each color.
  - Tapping balloons in the air—short sound instruments play on each tap, longer sounds play while balloon is in air, stopping at each tap.
  - Bouncing balls, rolling to partner, spinning and stopping.
  - Blowing soap bubbles—some play on burst, some on float.
- Divide into small groups and have children take turns conducting with chosen objects.

Variations:
- Find children's toys that can serve as sound stimuli (like pop guns, puppets that can be pushed out of a cone and pulled back in, tin chickens pecking corn, etc.)
- Use voice instead of percussion instruments. Use voice with percussion instruments (as in sing while soap bubble floats and play when it pops).
- Follow the popping of popcorn.

Music extension:
Look at cartoons with special attention to the sound accompaniment. Discuss the use of music to animate and accent the action in plays and films. Choose an action scene in a cartoon like one with the Road Runner or in a film like Charlie Chaplin's *Modern Times* (the factory scene). Watch several times without the sound and have kids create an accompanying percussion score. At the end, turn on the sound and listen to the "real" score.

Comments:
Music is an art form that moves through time. This is why the exercise of transferring a static visual image (as in, "play a chair") is difficult and is usually musically unsatisfying. In this exercise, the movement of the objects creates points of rest, release, accent, ascent, and descent that move through time in a similar way to music. Once again, the musical results of this exercise are not likely to be shared in a concert, but the challenge of unswerving attention waiting for the bubble to burst or popcorn to pop, the fun and surprise of it, the feeding of the capacity to "think strangely,"* and the playful partnership of eye and ear make this an exercise worth trying.

* Orff teacher Judith Thomas's marvelous expression used to describe one of many gifts of the Schulwerk.

31. RHYTHMIC NOTATION

Focus: Visual-Spatial Intelligence

Concept: Tracking

Activity:
- Choose three-dimensional objects that can stand for quarter notes ("ta") and eighth notes ("ta te"). Some examples:
  - Large pencil for "ta," two small ones for "ta te."
  - Large cup and two small ones.
  - Large action figure and two small ones.
- Collect at least four large figures and eight small ones.
- Line the four large ones in sight of the group and, moving from left to right, point to each while the group recites "ta." Invite them to repeat the rhythm four times without leader pointing.
- Invite them to continually repeat the rhythm while leader changes two small figures for one large one during the recitation. Group must respond accordingly. Leader continues to shift.
- As above, but remove one "ta" or two "ta te"s. Group must "conserve" the beat by leaving one beat of silence.
- Any of the above transferred to clapping or instruments.

Variations:
- Choose new leaders to manipulate the objects or work in partners.
- Select four or eight live people to be the figures. Standing straight stands for "ta," with legs apart for "ta te," and curved body (or crouched down or back to group) for rest. Each can change position after each phrase.

Music extension:
Sight-read written rhythms on cards or on the board using "ta," "ta te," rest. Notate nursery rhymes on paper or board.

Classroom application:
Discuss the parallels between reading music and reading words. (Tracking from left to right, B always sounds "B," ta always sounds "ta," you can make different combinations of words, you can make different combinations of rhythms, and so on.) Discuss the differences. (There are a lot more words than rhythmic values; "Tom goes to the store" and "To the store goes Tom" mean basically the same thing, but ♪♪♪♪♩ ¿ and ♪♪♩ ♩ ♩ mean something quite different in music.)

Comments:
Visual tracking is a key skill for both reading words and reading music. The eye must leap from the end of the line back to the beginning and, later, from the end of the line to the beginning of the next. This is one activity that is best not done in a circle.

In keeping with our imaginative approach, we enter the rather dry world of symbolic representation through a bit of fancy—cups, action figures, etc. The visual part of the brain is on all-systems alert, as a single moment of lost focus might place the "ta te" in the wrong place! This is also a great exercise to introduce the rest and the Piagetian concept of conservation—though we don't see it, the space where the object was remains and "the beat goes on."

SECTION VI:
THE BODILY-KINESTHETIC INTELLIGENCE

When Alfred North Whitehead warned that "you will come to grief as soon as you forget that your pupils have bodies," and Maria Montessori wrote that "the skill of man's hand is bound up with the development of his mind," they suggested that the body not only has its own form of intelligence, but that it is directly linked with our mental capacities as well. We reward those gifted with a bodily intelligence when it manifests in sports, but have an incomplete understanding of the many ways in which this gift may emerge and how essential it is to success and understanding in widely divergent fields. The bodily-kinesthetic intelligence can be defined as:

- The capacity to perceive and imitate the "dance" in all motion—human, animal, environmental (natural and mechanical)—and create our own movement expressions.
- The capacity to control and direct one's bodily motion, to carry and shift weight.
- The capacity to see meaning in gesture.
- The capacity to handle objects skillfully.
- The tendency to know the world through touch.

Isadora Duncan gives a succinct statement of the way such a person thinks:

If I could tell you what it is, I would not have danced it.

—Isadora Duncan

This intelligence manifests in dance, mime, acting, athletics, visual arts, crafts, invention, massage, car mechanics, manual labor, and, of course, music. The kinesthetic aspect of music is one of the qualities that separates it so markedly from the so-called academic subjects. Yet it is precisely the quality that qualifies it for a new/old paradigm of education. The deep understanding of music proceeds from the making of music—the Spanish word "to play music" is "tocar," which also means "touch." The hand speaks to the brain and carves out new neural pathways. The brain speaks back to the hand and builds a repertoire of intelligent, expressive, and efficient movements. Body and mind work hand in hand to build our musicality, which passes through the heart in both directions, we move and are moved, touch and are touched. Even if we don't play music, we are physically responding to it while listening, both inwardly and outwardly. Just watch the crowd at any concert; though the particular moves vary with the musical style, the impulse to move is shared.

All music requires some degree of kinesthetic intelligence—remembering the shapes in the fingers as one strums the guitar, mastering the motion of the bow, and controlling the flow of the breath. In addition to these inherent qualities, we need activities that give permission for the somatic approach to learning to be as valid and authentic as an ear or pattern approach. The following exercises highlight the physical aspect of entering music and sustaining interest.

32. FRAME DRUM TECHNIQUE

Focus: Kinesthetic Intelligence

Concept: Sound/touch interplay

Activity:
- Explore possible ways of striking the drum and note the resultant sounds: rubbing drum, striking with knuckles, tapping fingers, shaking hand on the drum skin, thumb only, and so on.
- Explore specific techniques on the frame drum as follows:
    - Holding drum perpendicular to floor in left hand, strike edge of the drum with a downward motion of the thumb. The wrist should flick and thumb release from the drum to produce a resonant "dum" tone.
    - Keeping thumb in place, strike with a flicked downward motion and release of the pointer finger on the edge of the drum to produce a "tak" sound.
    - Strike with the whole hand in the center of the drum and keep hand on skin after striking to get a muted sound.
    - Strike with all four fingers flicking upward on upper end of the drum to get an alternate (often not as resonant) "dum" sound.
- Create and practice a simple pattern using all strokes.
- Explore different intensities of playing (hard/soft/fast/slow, etc.)

Variations:
- Hold the drum in a different way and explore new techniques and finger position: for example, Egyptian tar.
- Balance drum between legs.

Music extensions:
Watch Glen Velez and Layne Redmond videos.

Classroom application:
Grip a pencil in different ways and note the change in the handwriting.

Comments:
Frame drum is the generic term given to describe a drum in which the width of the wood frame is less than the diameter of the skin head. It is generally held in the hand and played with the hand, hence, its alternate name of hand drum. The frame drum is one of the most universal instruments, found in distinct forms in many cultures worldwide. It is also one of the oldest known instruments, seen in sculptures and wall paintings from over four thousand years ago, often played by women.

This lesson is a bridge from the romance of freewheeling musical investigation to the nuts and bolts of expressive technique. If the children are unduly frustrated, it may mean that they're not emotionally or physically ready to tackle this task. Consider more free play, reducing the range of strokes, waiting for an older age, or persevering with gentle reminders that anything worth learning takes time to master. The key point here is that sound and touch are inseparable: not only must the ear hear the difference between beautiful and less-beautiful tones, but the hand (or arm or foot or breath) must also learn how to create and control them. The process of refining musical expression can come from either direction, i.e., the teacher might say, "Play as softly as you can," and the hand will intuitively strike more gently, or the teacher might say, "Play with the smallest and lightest strokes you can," and the resultant sound will be quieter. This is not news to musicians, who spend a good part of any lesson or class adjusting, correcting, and evoking particular physical gestures and techniques.

Since numerous books, videos, and recordings cover specific percussion techniques, I simply include this one basic example to highlight the profound connection between the musical and kinesthetic intelligences.

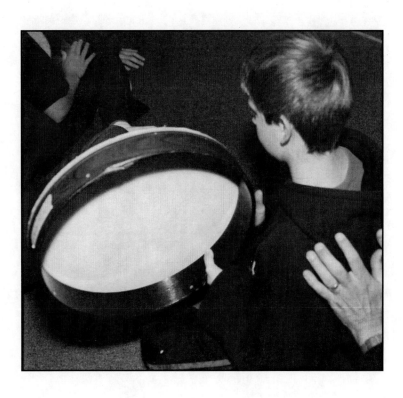

33. BACK DRUMMING

Focus: Kinesthetic Intelligence

Concept: Interlocking rhythms

Activity:
- All seated in a circle faced to the right, every other person with a percussion instrument. Those without instruments (number ones) put hands on the back of the person in front (number twos).
- A number one begins playing a pattern on partner's back; partner plays that rhythm on percussion instrument.

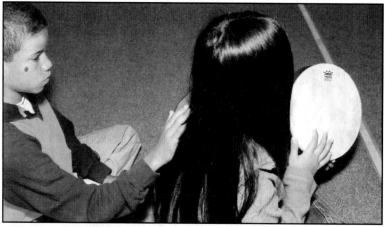

- Next pair in the circle repeat above, fitting their new rhythm into the one already playing.
- Continue as above around the circle until all are playing.
- Ones stop, twos continue. Ones find vocal ostinati to add to the piece.
- Twos stop; ones continue. After a time, twos come back in, ones resume drumming on back, each pair dropping out one at a time around the circle.

Variations:
- Ones dance instead of sing when they drop out.
- When twos re-enter, they create new pattern. Ones match that pattern on back.
- Switch ones and twos.

Classroom application:
Students pair up as above. Partner one figures a way to give a math problem on the back (touching two fingers, then seven fingers, partner two has to add up and give the answer) or draws a shape that the partner must identify (circle, triangle, square, etc.) or draws on paper or traces on the back of a letter that the partner must identify or write.

Comments:
The idea for this piece came from reading an account of how West African drum masters sometimes taught rhythms to their students by drumming on their back. Instead of sharing this with my students as an interesting ethnic experience, I decided to actually try it with them. We are accustomed to learning rhythms through the eye, the ear, and the tongue (through language), but learning them from touch is a markedly different experience!

From the exercise came the idea of putting it into form and creating a piece out of it. The idea of the ones dropping out and creating vocal ostinati was both musically inspired and practical, as some of the twos began to complain of "grooves being worn in their backs" by the repetitive rhythms! Once again, the circle formation serves us well in creating an easy structure for adding rhythms.

34. BLIND PLAYING

Focus: Kinesthetic Intelligence

Concept: Hand intelligence

Set-up: Kids seated with instruments in the circle with matching instruments spread out in the center of the circle.

Activity:
One child blindfolded or with eyes closed in the center. A game leader points to someone in the circle to play an instrument (for example, a triangle). The blindfolded child tries to find the triangle by shape and then tests it by sound, improvising together with the child in the circle who is playing. If incorrect, the blindfolded child tries again to find the triangle. When correct, the child playing in the circle becomes the next in the center, and the blindfolded child removes the blindfold and chooses the next person in the circle to play.

Variations:
One instrument per person and its pair in the center of the circle. One student is blindfolded, another mixes up the instruments in the circle and the blindfolded student tries to find the companion instrument by touch. While searching, all play their instruments, getting louder when the searcher is close, softer when farther way.

Music extension:
Research famous sight-impaired musicians: Art Tatum, Rahsaan Roland Kirk, George Shearing, Stevie Wonder, Jose Feliciano, Ray Charles, Reverend Gary Davis, Blind Tom, etc. Discuss why there are more blind jazz and blues musicians than classical musicians.

Classroom application:
A version of this technique is commonly used in science museums: identification of an object through touch. Play an identification game using classroom materials.

Comments:
The idea for this game came from my colleague Sofía López-Ibor, who learned a similar game in Ghana about sorting flip-flops thrown into the middle of the circle. It requires a tactile memory and hands sensitive to size, shape, and temperature. In a world of dishwashers, food processors, and automatic garage-door openers, the hands of both children and adults are beginning to atrophy and lose their capacity for a sensory entanglement with the world. Aesthetics, so central to art, comes from sensory engagement. This game serves to reawaken our slumbering hands.

Closing the eyes is always a useful strategy in re-perceiving the world—especially the aural world. The list of accomplished blind musicians makes it clear that the visual aspect of music can be of secondary importance—especially in musical cultures based more on the ear than the eye. Even in note-reading styles, feeling where the notes are on the instrument is essential to success. The young recorder player looking cross-eyed down the pipe must constantly be reminded to feel where the holes are rather than look.

Through the simple act of closing the eyes, the energy shifts, and the tactile element becomes more prominent. This exercise is most interesting musically with a melodic instrument like the xylophone or piano.

35. ACCOMPANYING DANCERS

Focus: Kinesthetic Intelligence

Concept: Dance/music interplay

Activity:
- Brainstorm a list of movement verbs, such as walk, hop, slither, prance, and a second list of adverbs, such as quickly, slowly, sloppily, sadly. Write each word on a file card: one color card for verbs and another color for adverbs.
- Form partners, each pair choosing two cards—one from the verb pile, one from the adverb. One partner creates a dance based on the combination of the words (hop slowly, prance sadly, etc.) while the other accompanies the dancer with percussion instruments.
- Have three or four groups of partners perform simultaneously, with musicians following dancers. Dancers start with starting shape and intuit when to end.

Variations:
- Partners as above with dancers improvising freely and musicians following.
- Reverse—dancers move to musicians' improvisation.
- In a large group setting (say three dancers and many musicians), assign one type of instrument to each dancer. Dancers move and freeze, with musicians following.

Music extension:
- Listen to dance music and imagine the dancing.
- Watch a dance video with the sound off and imagine the music. Choose a specific dance and discuss the interplay between musicians and dancers.

Classroom application:
Discuss the question of which comes first—the egg or the chicken. Apply to a discussion of dance and music.

Comments:
Did music arise as an aural response to dance? Did dance come into being as a visual activation of music? These are ancient questions that still resonate today. In some traditions, the dancer determines some of the direction of the music (as in Balinese gamelan), in some, the musician cues the dancer, and in many, there is a symbiotic relationship of equal influence.

This exercise plays with some of that dynamic in its raw form. It could have been placed also in the Visual-Spatial Intelligence category as musicians need to watch carefully to translate a form of moving notation to sound. This overlap of categories proves once again that these are provisional highlights of provisional distinctions of intelligence. In the real human brain and our real experience of life, these interconnections are the rule, not the exception.

36. MOVING WITH INSTRUMENTS

Focus: Kinesthetic Intelligence

Concept: Moving with object as stimulus

Activity:
- Explore freely improvised movement with instrument in hand. The weight, shape, and quality of the instrument becomes the impetus and focus for movement. Sounding the instrument while moving is an option.
- Move with the instrument balanced on different body parts.
- Move around the instrument on the floor.

Variations:
- Face a partner with a similar instrument and imitate in mirror movement.
- Stand behind the partner and imitate in shadow movement.
- Choreograph a set sequence combining ideas of others with like instruments.

Music extension:
Watch the video of the show *Stomp.*

Comments:
Carl Orff's first experiments in restoring the unity of music and movement to West European culture took place in the 1920s in Munich, Germany. There, young women training to be dancers moved with hand drums, finger cymbals and other small percussion, integrating the instruments into their dance and dancing the musical ideas played on the instruments. This kind of activity follows the previous idea of movement enacting music and music reflecting movement, only this time, with the mover and musician being the same person. ☺

SECTION VII:
THE PERSONAL INTELLIGENCES

By elevating emotional and social skills to intelligences, Gardner both recognizes that these can be gifts of birth and human potentials that can be developed and trained in a somewhat similar fashion to language, math, music, and more. He calls them the "intrapersonal" and "interpersonal" intelligences. Though they are clearly linked, they are also distinct enough to merit separate consideration. The intrapersonal intelligence can be described as:
- The capacity to locate and build a sense of self.
- The capacity to monitor behavior and develop self-control.
- The capacity to recognize, name, analyze, and discriminate between feelings and emotions.
- The capacity to be self-aware of personal patterns, tendencies, learning styles, obstacles, and gifts, and to set personal goals, make resolutions, and strive for self-improvement.

Actors able to read, imitate, and create multiple moods and personalities are keyed into the forms of character and feeling the way a poet might tune to words and a musician to notes. Storytellers, playwrights, and novelists must likewise have a good feel for mood and character.

The connection with story and self is a profound one. One of the primary strategies for building self is through stories, both formal and informal. Witness young children playing doctor or cops and robbers—they are trying on different roles, acting out different possibilities. Likewise, those who are told many stories and read stories have a wide palette from which to paint their emerging personality. One of the strategies for reform of convicts is to send storytellers in to tell them stories and eventually get them to write their own. Their inability to tell coherent stories about themselves and imagine stories about their future is one of the signs of a self that was not wholly formed and must be re-formed through the process of storytelling. Therapists of various schools likewise share in common the telling and re-telling of our personal stories, extracting new meanings and shades of meaning in an attempt to re-vision self and further develop our intrapersonal intelligence.

The interpersonal intelligence can be described as:
- The capacity to perceive, react to, and empathize with feelings, states, and needs of others.
- The capacity to recognize and remember people.
- The capacity to perceive and react to the dynamics of relationship in social encounters.
- The capacity to work with and for the group.

These capacities are necessary in effective parenting, teaching, social work, politics, human relations, administration, business management, coaching, medicine, law, personal services, military command, and, of course, music.

All the activities offered in this book demand a high degree of interpersonal intelligence. Consider revisiting them all from a social perspective. The simple act (which is not so simple after all!) of making music together requires awareness of others around you, a sense of offering oneself to the group, and blending one's voice in the fabric of the greater whole. The additional invitation to *create* music together increases the responsibility to listen, share ideas, give, and take until arriving at some sense of agreement, which is manifested in the delight of shared creation.

The intrapersonal intelligence is likewise given attention in this style of work, from the opening name games to the intimate character of the small group that invites each person to be known, to the frequent opportunity to improvise and express one's feelings and thoughts in a variety of mediums.

Once again, it is impossible to isolate this intelligence and claim any one exercise as its prime activator. The following activities tend toward the drama and storytelling end of the Schulwerk, for it is through stories and their enactment in drama that we build a sense of self and learn our most important social lessons.

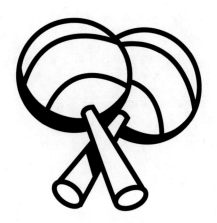

37. INSTRUMENTS AS PROPS

Focus: Intrapersonal Intelligence

Concept: Dramatic imagination

Activity:
- All transform their instrument into something else. Some examples:
  - Hand drums can become steering wheels, soup bowls, frisbees (but don't throw them!).
  - Recorders can become telescopes, pepper mills, pool cues.
  - Agogo bells can become telephones, wine goblets, binoculars.
- Create a skit with a group based on instrumental props.

Variations:
Create a spontaneous skit in random groups without planning.

Classroom application:
- Apply the above idea to classroom materials.
- Turn classroom materials into musical instruments. Some examples:
  - Rulers with one part overhanging the edge of the desk that are plucked.
  - Spiral-bound notebooks played with pencils like guiros.
  - Staple-removers played like castanets.
  - Overturned (empty) wastebaskets played like drums.

Comments: The child's naturally imaginative mind loves to play with objects as described above. Part of the journey to adulthood seems to be to learn the serious and proper use of each object. By balancing that learning with an invitation to play with objects unconventionally, several important lessons are taught:
- Children's intuitive delight in playing is given an adult stamp of approval and included in the formal definition of learning.
- The excitement of diverse perspectives and the importance of each child's contribution is acknowledged.
- The capacity to appreciate metaphor—one thing standing for something else—is given a foundation on a physical plane.

While children—and adults—certainly need to learn proper technique, care, and function of each tool in their field, some time spent exploring unconventional uses of material adds greatly to the creative ambience of any class. Most important, it's a great deal of fun. These improvisations are invariably the most exciting of any!

We've put on many a delightful play in which the instrument became the prop, doubling as a visual gag and a musical accompaniment. Eating scenes are particularly effective: "food" brought out on frame drum platters, ratchet pepper mills, rainstick bottles of wine, clave chopsticks, afuche ice cream cones and more. Bon appetit!

38. PERCUSSIVE STORYTELLING

Focus: Intrapersonal Intelligence

Concept: Musical storytelling

Activity:
Each person shares a short story from his or her personal life, accompanying the telling with a percussion instrument. The accompaniment can comment on the text, provide an underlying beat or ostinato, offer a musical interlude with no words, or combine all these ideas.

Variations:
- Think the story and tell it with percussion only.
- Tell a personal story to a partner and have the partner accompany the story.

Classroom application:
- Have select students accompany a story that the teacher is reading.
- Create a score to a simple fairy tale: *The Three Billy Goats Gruff*; *The Three Little Pigs*; *Goldilocks and the Three Bears*; etc.

Comments:
Many modern storytellers borrow from various traditional practices and tell stories accompanied by drumming. The drum can set the mood, determine the tempo, offer refreshment from words, and accent and punctuate phrases. This activity, which could also easily slip into the linguistic category, explores the relationships between words and sound while simultaneously revealing something of each person to the group. The instrument serves as an aural mask, freeing the storyteller to move beyond self-consciousness and to consider sharing something more intimate than usual. It also can reveal more of the story (and hence the inner life of the teller) through the power of improvised sound.

39. PREFERRED INSTRUMENTS

Focus: Intrapersonal Intelligence

Concept: Self-study

Activity:
- Each person chooses her or his favorite percussion instrument (taking turns and sharing as needed) and improvises or works out a short solo.
- Based on the nature of the solo, others comment on what they imagine attracted the student to that instrument (it's loud; it's quiet; you can play fast sounds; etc.). Soloist tries to articulate why he or she chose that instrument.
- Continue with other soloists.

Variations:
Each group creates an improvisation based on the blending of the qualities each person likes about the instrument. For example, two people may choose a drum, one for its strong sound, the other for its circular shape. Each highlights that quality in a combined improvisation.

Music extension:
Study the lives of composers or interview local musicians to discover and discuss how they chose which instrument to play (or how it chose them).

Classroom application:
Imagine what instruments a favorite character in a story would like.

Comments:
A key feature of multiple intelligence theory is that we are intelligent in many ways. Equally important is the notion that we each have a preferred intelligence or unique blend of preferred intelligences, those mysterious impulses that send us toward our college major. Though it should now be clear that all seven (and perhaps more) intelligences are always working together and that we can never devote ourselves exclusively to one without drawing from the others, we do indeed choose to devote more energy to a few select fields. What is true on the macro level is also true on the micro level. To say our preferred intelligence is musical is not enough: we then must discover which *aspect* of musicality is our gift. If the brain works in general, interactive ways, it also gets very specific. From music we whittle down from a choice of vocal music, instrumental music, music theory, music composition, music arranging, music history. If instrumental music is our thing, we whittle down more to percussion, strings, aerophones. If we pick aerophones, then we choose from saxophone, clarinet, trumpet, bagpipe, flute; then alto sax, tenor sax, soprano sax, baritone sax. From there, we might get specific about which brand of alto sax, which reed, and so forth.

In the big picture of education, we might say that school exists for a twofold purpose. The first is to give each intelligence a chance to grow in a carefully tended and cultivated garden, and to give every student sufficient exposure and training to develop a solid foundation in each intelligence. Here the direction opens outward, focusing on breadth of exposure, and aims toward the community, making sure that all children have equal opportunity to develop their inherent genius in each intelligence. The second is to help every student discover his or her preferred intelligences, from the macro level of the first-grader showing a propensity for language, to the micro level of the doctoral student researching grammatical patterns of the Ainu people in a specific region of Northern Japan.

The Orff class is built on the principle of the generalist and gives young children a broad exposure to an immense variety of mediums, musical styles, and instrumental types. We purposely guard against the glockenspiel specialist and insist that students try all sides of the musical picture—singing in one piece, dancing in another, playing recorder or drums, or the bass part or the lead melody in succeeding pieces. When playing the same piece several times with students, we switch parts for each playing. This has proven to be an excellent principle of building a musical foundation—but only up to a point. The student who is serious about continuing must begin to specialize, probably outside of the Orff class in private lessons and community ensembles. The process of reflecting on what instrument (or instruments) calls to you is an essential part of the total picture.

Though it is enough to simply feel what calls to you, this exercise suggests the possibility of using language to clarify why and of using the instrument as a tool for self-reflection. It does not aim to elicit any therapeutic breakthrough, but to simply suggest one step further in the intrapersonal realm using instrumental preference as a guide. In my own life, I found myself attracted to the Bulgarian bagpipe. My understanding of that urge was having a tool to express a part of myself not available in the sweet tones of the glockenspiel. Though I've lost many friends as a result, it has been valuable to recognize that part of my nature. (I've also taken up the accordion, which has alienated the other half of my friends. Though this exercise may be valuable intrapersonally, it can be a real disaster *inter*personally!)

CODA:
THE DRUMMERS IN GOLDEN GATE PARK

Having written the text to the last game in this book, I took a much needed break and set out into Golden Gate Park near my house. It was a beautiful spring day, and I had no sooner stepped into the park when I heard the familiar drumming from "hippie hill" near the children's playground. Every day (and especially popular on Sundays), drummers of all sizes, shapes, ages, races, sexes, and talent converge at the bottom of the hill and begin playing. They bring congas and djembes and dumbeks and surdos and talking drums and frame drums and claves and bells and shakers and whistles and just about any soundmaker you can imagine. Around them people dance, throw frisbees, juggle fire, wave banners, practice capoeira, or just sit, watch, and listen. There is no leader, no formal repertoire of pieces, no clearly marked **A** sections and **B** sections. Someone simply begins a groove and others join in. People spontaneously take turns soloing, change their pattern, or just stay happily in the mix. Sometimes the beat accelerates or the pattern changes or it simply fades out at its own pace, as if the drums themselves have finished speaking that piece of their message for the day. A few moments of silence and a new one arises and off they go again. What are these people doing? What brings them to the drum? What brings them together to drum? What does the drum bring to them? What does the drumming bring to the spring day?

These people are not drumming to improve their math scores, though the patterns, subpatterns, and countless variations will wear deep grooves in their pattern-making brain. They're not there to wield power, though the beats are like push-ups for the soul that strengthen their inner spiritual power. They're not there to meet people or flirt or display themselves, though twinkling eyes and warm embraces may be an afterthought when the drums have stopped. They're not there to accomplish something or build their resume or go from green-belt drumming to black-belt. They're not there to earn free miles or improve their tennis game or get in touch with the inner masculinity or powerful femininity. They're not there to win friends or influence people or to upgrade their software or to have a nice day or any of the other tired clichés of contemporary life.

They come because their spirits thirst for communion. When they play, the rhythms hit below the belt of the ego that strives for attainment or self-improvement, awakens the liver, hits the solar plexus, drains the blood away from the head and toward the pit of the stomach. When they hit the groove and are carried along its current, they are *connected*—to their own drum, to their own rhythm, to the other drums and other rhythms, to themselves, to each other, to the people responding to it, to the nearby cypress trees, to the day itself. They sit at the center of a powerful cross, its vertical dimension rooted in the earth and aspiring to the heavens, its horizontal holding the people sitting on the bench next to them, the dog romping in the field, the pleasure of Sunday in the park.

How marvelous that this happens! The effect is immediate and electric—and accessible to anyone who takes the time to do it. Most of the drummers probably practice simply by playing a lot, alone and with others. There are no methods books or scales or drills. There are no auditions to pass or fail, no conservatory training required, no national standards to check off, no union dues to pay, no assessment procedures. All you need to do is listen, join in, and let the hands speak for the heart.

All cultures of all times need these fundamental experiences and need them often. Those cultures that have had the wisdom to maintain such traditions have carried forth intricate drumming traditions that not only heal in general ways, but in very specific ways as well, each rhythm attending to a different organ in the body and quality of the psyche. When we understand—as many today do—that technological progress and comfort are not the only criteria for assessing human culture, the various "third world" cultures become the "first worlds" of ritual, tradition, and community, and we flock to West Africa, Brazil, India, Bali, or the Bulgarian countryside to learn from them.

The drummers in Golden Gate Park are less sophisticated, more random, and less powerful in some ways than these highly developed traditions. But in the drummers' unconscious attraction to drumming and their need to gather, we can hear the voice of the spirit itself demanding a place in an upperworld crowded with soulless machines, overly abstract thought, a massive appetite to consume and possess, an obsession with winning and success. Whether officially banned by slavemasters, or actively repressed by some religious groups, or abandoned and neglected by corporate mentality, the drums will always return to have their say.

The spirit of the games presented here is to consciously bring drumming into the world of the school, not as tools to achieve something else or as a means to attain prefabricated standards, but as playmates and companions ready to help us speak what needs to be spoken. When Gardner's work entered mainstream education, many educators rightfully worried that we now would have seven IQ tests instead of one. Nothing would be more disappointing to me than to discover that someone had used the ideas in this book to "make the kids smarter" seven different ways. These ideas are but convenient ways to think more deeply about how humans learn; how the brain, heart, and hands work; how music works; how the creative imagination might catch fire; how the community might actively grow; and how the souls and spirits of children might find a voice.

In schools, homes, parks, and office buildings nationwide, may the drums be sounded!

Doug Goodkin

Doug Goodkin teaches music and movement to young people from the age of three to fourteen at The San Francisco School, where he has taught since 1975. He is an internationally recognized practitioner of Orff-Schulwerk, teaching Orff courses throughout North America, Europe, and Australia. He is the director of the Mills College Orff Certification Course in Oakland, California, and teaches his own summer course on jazz and Orff-Schulwerk.

Doug has published numerous articles on Orff in contemporary culture and is author of *Play, Sing & Dance: An Introduction to Orff Schulwerk* as well as an author of the Macmillan/McGraw-Hill textbook series *Share the Music*. He is a founding member of the Orff-based adult performing group Xephyr. Doug is known for his innovative application of Orff-Schulwerk across various disciplines, particularly language arts, jazz, and multicultural music.